PHOTO BY RENEE SOLOWAY

Bette Ziegler (left) and Jane Seskin

Jane Seskin, a free-lance writer on the contemporary scene, lectures throughout the country on women's issues. The author of many books and articles, her next book will be: *Conversations with Women over Sixty-five*.

Bette Ziegler has had her plays produced off-off Broadway and is the author of two novels. She teaches creative writing in Caldwell, New Jersey. A psychology major, she graduated from Fairleigh Dickinson University.

OLDER WOMEN/ YOUNGER MEN

OLDER WOMEN/ YOUNGER MEN

*Jane Seskin
and Bette Ziegler*

1979
ANCHOR PRESS/DOUBLEDAY
GARDEN CITY, NEW YORK

The Anchor Press edition is the first publication of OLDER WOMEN/ YOUNGER MEN.

Anchor Press edition: 1979

Library of Congress Cataloging in Publication Data

Seskin, Jane.
  Older women/younger men.

  Bibliography: p. 142
  Includes index.
  1. Interpersonal relations—Case studies. 2. Unmarried couples—
Case studies. 3. Middle aged women—United States—Case studies.
4. Young men—United States—Case studies. 5. Marriage—United States
—Case studies. I. Ziegler, Bette, joint author. II. Title.
HM132.S474   301.41
ISBN: 0-385-13698-6
Library of Congress Catalog Card Number 78–69667

ACKNOWLEDGMENTS

This book is about those people living, loving, and growing in a new type of relationship. It couldn't have been written without the men and women who let us into their lives and spent countless hours filling out questionnaires and talking into our tape recorder. We are grateful to them for allowing their thoughts to appear on these pages. We came to know many of them well and appreciate the trust they placed in us. To preserve privacy, we have changed names and cities of origin and altered physical descriptions.

In addition, the following people made invaluable contributions to this project, and without them this book would not have been the same. We are indebted to Dr. Michael Carrera, Dr. Albert Ellis, Janet Gifford, Sam Julty, Thomas Kline, Mildred Klingman, Dr. Louis Lieberman, Dr. Wayne Myers, Nena O'Neill, Dr. Arline Rubin, Dr. Penelope Russianoff, Dr. Leah Schaefer, and Barry B. Wolff for generously giving of their time, information, and insights.

Special mention to Meredith Bernstein, Marie D. Brown, Gladys Dobelle, Jeanne Flaks, Carolyn Goudsmit, Janet Harris, Patricia Hinkley, Margo Husin, Pat Posner, Annette, Samuel and Stuart Rosenblum, Vicki Rubin, Ellen and Adam Schmalholz, Don Wigal, and Laurie, Scott, and Herman Ziegler for their continuous support and encouragement.

CONTENTS

INTRODUCTION

A few months ago, one of our friends, age thirty-three, left her husband for a twenty-one-year-old graduate student. Another friend, a thirty-six-year-old divorcee with two preteenagers, living in a Long Island suburb, began sharing her home with her son's twenty-five-year-old art teacher. And the eldest son of a family we knew moved in with his mother's friend from college after she was granted her divorce.

It appeared to us that something new and unconventional was happening. Could it be that what had formerly been underground and whispered about to the accompaniment of raised eyebrows was much more common than we had ever expected? We began to discuss this coupling with friends, associates, and professional colleagues and found that everyone had a story to tell or knew someone who was involved in this type of relationship. Intrigued by what we heard and observed, we decided to explore the subject in greater depth.

We sought out men and women who felt that the older-woman/younger-man relationships they were involved in had significantly affected their lives. The subjects for this book responded to ads placed in newspapers and magazines asking for people involved in serious, long-term relationships. A ripple effect occurred as these people referred us to others. In addition, we interviewed personal friends and acquaintances who met the same criteria.

Through questionnaires, tapes, personal interviews, and group dialogues, we assembled the material for the bulk of this book. We also asked numerous psychologists, sex therapists, sociologists, and writers in the field of human behavior to comment on this trend.

How do we define the phrases "older woman" and "younger man"? The word "older" to one person might mean twenty years; to another, it could be a difference of six months. The term "younger" carried the same subjective feelings. What really constituted a significant age difference? Was there a definitive time line that separated generations? And if there was, was it chronological, physical, or imagined? And finally what difference, if any, did it make?

The more we talked to people, the more we began to observe a double standard of aging. As men grow older, they are thought to be more attractive—seasoned and exciting. They are certainly viewed as more desirable. Men, it is thought, not only age well but grow better with age. Men are "distinguished" with added years, whereas women only age. As a woman grows older, she does her best to disguise it. A woman over thirty, asked her age, often hesitates and then frequently subtracts a couple of years before answering. Traditionally, women have been taught to lie, and the lie is never-ending.

Lynn Fontanne, who is now ninety, has said that when her husband, Alfred Lunt, died, in 1977, he thought she was a year younger than he was. In fact, she was almost five years older. Her reasoning? "I lied in the beginning because I was afraid he wouldn't like me."[1]

Along with our attitudes toward aging, we are still locked into traditional role models. The dewy-eyed, virginal look is coveted in a woman; in a man it is to be avoided at all costs. Very few women want an inexperienced man; an experienced woman though, is advised to play it down. Women are cautioned to be assertive but not aggressive, because that is a masculine trait. They are fighting for equal rights in the boardroom and in the bedroom, yet they must still battle to remain "acceptable" when they are the pursuer and older.

It is a "seventies phenomenon" that successful middle-class men in their forties and fifties tend to make drastic changes in their life-styles. To affirm their physical prowess and bolster sagging egos, they often turn to younger women for sexual reassurance and emotional comfort and support.

A couple in which the man is obviously older than the woman might quickly be categorized by statements such as

"Aha, he's got money" or "She's looking for a father." The older-woman/younger-man pairing cannot be put out of your mind so easily, because it is the exception rather than the rule, and therefore, provokes far more questions and comment. (What is the attraction? How did they ever get together? Is something wrong with the man? Is the woman overly protective? Does she appear young and especially attractive for her age? Does he look older? Is Oedipus rearing his ugly head?)

Studies indicate that two out of three women experience widowhood in their lifetime. In addition, divorce and legal separation are on the upswing; and more and more women are opting for the single life. It seems that today's older woman is in a double bind. Not only aren't there as many eligible men available as there are women, but often her male peers are not interested in her—because of her age. More often than not, this woman is self-supporting and has been touched in some way by the women's movement. Although she is now moving with the times, she is still beset by social and physical loneliness After all, how many times a week can she have dinner with "the girls"? And yet, for the majority of older women, the thought never enters their mind that they have another option: that there is no reason they should restrict themselves to the same norms of social behavior they held when growing up, and that what is good for their male counterparts can also be good for them.

We have known since Kinsey that the older-woman/younger-man pairing has physiological advantages. In his two studies *Sexual Behavior in the Human Male* and *Sexual Behavior in the Human Female*; Kinsey stated that one of the major causes of unhappiness is the difference in the strength of the sex drive between men and women.

Men have a much higher orgastic rate than women as teenagers and manifest a slow, linear decline with age. Women show a slight rise in their twenties and maintain this level until their late fifties. The curves of orgastic behavior are on the average far apart in early adulthood, and narrowly apart in late middle and early old age. In the early years of marriage, men may constantly pressure women for sex and experience frustration in her lesser interests. But over the years most females become less inhibited and develop an interest in sexual relations which they may then maintain until they are in their fifties and even sixties. However, by then the responses of the average male may have dropped considerably so that his interest in coitus has sharply declined. In the later years his descending sex drive may cross with her more or less constant sex drive and eventually she may become more desirous of sex than he.[2]

Gail Sheehy, in *Passages*, describes this configuration as that of a "Sexual Diamond." "Men and women," Sheehy states,

at the age of emancipation start out alike. In the twenties they begin moving apart in every way: in sexual capacity and availability for sex (especially once the woman's reproductive potential is tapped), in social roles that are massively different and that also favor different personality characteristics, and in the overall sense of themselves. By the late thirties and early forties, the distance across the diamond is at its greatest. Males and females are exhibiting the most strikingly dissimilar aspects of their sexual capacities. At the same time, they are called upon to admit the sexually opposite sides of their natures, which are so frighteningly unfamiliar. In the fifties, they both go into a sexual involution, which eventually brings them back together in the unisex of old age.[3]

Sheehy, like Kinsey, hypothesizes that many women exhibit their sexual potential most strongly at the same time that their husband's sexual incentive is declining. What is left is a vicious circle—the midlife woman actively seeking satisfaction of her now uninhibited sexual desires from a man who, wary in the presence of any naked demand, goes into voluntary retreat. Sheehy states: Even when contrary to their own individual experience, women have accepted the mythological profiles of the eighteen-year-old boy who's a prisoner of his hormones and of the young girl reproductively ready but who won't arrive sexually for ten or fifteen more years. Many women thus willed themselves into sexual dormancy, and Sheehy asks: How could nature be so perverse?[4]

Dr. Mary Jane Sherfey, in her study *The Evolution and Nature of Female Sexuality in Relation to Psychoanalytic Theory*, suggests that the forceful suppression of women's inordinate sexual drive was a prerequisite to the dawn of every modern civilization and almost every living culture. She suggests that this primitive sexual drive was too strong, too susceptible to the fluctuating extremes of an impelling, aggressive eroticism, to withstand the disciplined requirements of a settled family life. Dr. Sherfey feels that women may well have an insatiable sex drive, like the sex drive of certain female primates who have an anatomy much like ours, and she emphasizes the effects of pregnancy on the American female's loss of sexual inhibition, stating that when the woman completes her child-bearing years, usually in her early thirties, she's at her fullest sexual availability.[5]

Not until these so-called "primitive" drives were gradually brought under control by rigidly enforced social codes could family life become the stabilizing and creative crucible from which modern man could emerge. Barbara Seaman has said that it seems only common sense to suppose that, in the interests of establishing paternity, an orderly family life, the descent of property, and so on, it was necessary to curb the woman's sex drive and encourage her to be monogamous. And surely one way to do this was to make sex unsatisfactory for her.[6]

Women, then, have had a long history and ample reason for hiding, abdicating, and negating their natural sexuality.

Seventy-five years ago, a woman could expect to live until she was about fifty. Today, her life expectancy has increased by twenty-five years. According to the 1977 Census Bureau report, there are more than three times as many female formerly marrieds and widows aged forty-five or older than there are male. For every five formerly married women there are three formerly-married men. How, then, do these newly single people get back into the social mainstream? And how will the single woman cope when, according to the numbers, she finds herself almost indelibly tagged "extra"?

A majority of people tend to follow the dating patterns established in their high school and college years: women choosing men from among their peer age group or upperclassmen, men choosing women of their own age or younger. The college senior of twenty-one would date a college freshman of eighteen, and it would be perfectly acceptable. And if she was beautiful and sexy, he'd score points. She'd score points also, because he was older, more mature, and had "been around." A mutual acceptance system prescribed a firmly fixed dating pattern in terms of age: women look up, and men look down, when forming social relationships. It is almost an automatic reflex.

> I'd never really been attracted to older men, but felt it was my only choice. My husband of twelve years was fifteen years older than me. I suffered terrible unhappiness for almost all the marriage because of feeling young and dumb.
>
> Ruth M., now a forty-six-year-old divorcee.

Telescope twenty years. The man is in his early forties; the woman is forty. Both are formerly married and are once again in the dating world. The man still dates women his own age and younger. The woman's circle of available men are her own age and older. In theory, the dating pattern hasn't changed. Men are still dating women younger than themselves. The major difference is that now the age range may vary anywhere from two to over twenty years younger. And women, faced with an ever dwindling number of men, have opted for loneliness rather than broadening their horizons and questioning their definitions of what constitutes an eligible man.

Women who always date men older than themselves and automatically exclude anyone younger without giving a thought to the man's emotional maturity, business acumen, or social sophistication are in all probability affected by the same myth that says taller is better, older is stronger, et cetera. We were reminded of this when a very petite lady of thirty-five told us that she had always gone out with much younger men and hadn't really given it much thought. Since she always had to look up to them (they were all over six feet tall), she never considered them as being younger!

Habitually, many women have thought of themselves as less than men, so what they wanted from a man was *more*; only in this way could they be complete. Added years on the male's side meant greater maturity, greater chance for success and recognition. These bonus points conferred status to the woman on his arm. But now that women and men are entering the job market in equal numbers and competing for the same rewards, women are beginning to look for the exact things that men have for centuries wanted from their women. *They want to be complimented; they want to be stroked; they want to allow their sexuality full rein; they want to be told how exciting and wonderful they are. And they want what people often want when they hit middle age: they want their youth!* A man their age has always had freedom of choice; the pool of available women is limitless. Only now are there concrete signs that the situation is beginning to be the same for women. The walls of the double standard are cracking, and the bricks are falling down.

Ashley Montagu, the noted anthropologist, believes women have *never* been given equal opportunities with men to develop their capacities. He says the opportunities for the development of their intelligence and tribal skills were severely restricted by what was traditionally considered permissible to women; they were prejudged rather than fairly judged; and they were condemned to a servitude from which they could never emerge unless granted the opportunity to do so.

Whether the opportunity was granted or it was seized, there is no doubt that women have turned a corner. The rise of the many liberation movements—in particular, the women's movement—has altered the self-concepts of our present generation away from passive acceptance of traditionally defined roles and norms.[7]

The feminist movement has contributed to the increase of older-woman/younger-man relationships because it has encouraged women to be more daring and more willing to take a chance in areas where they wouldn't have taken chances before. The movement has helped women to think of themselves as more autonomous, freer persons and therefore willing to risk making a choice that may not be particularly popular. Our view of sex roles has changed in recent times: *who* the woman is in terms of *her* accomplishments, power, and influence (attributes formerly ascribed chiefly to males) have now become socially desirable for women. Current changes in sexual attitudes can be seen as a natural outgrowth of social conditions in which earlier normative restrictions no longer hold.

Divorced from her oriental-doctor husband after the worldwide success of her first novel, *Fear of Flying*, Erica Jong has said: "My second husband was very supportive to me in my work. He was a kind of daddy figure. He was eight and a half years older, a doctor. It was the kind of marriage women make in their early twenties. Then, when you've proved yourself in your own career and feel secure, you can marry a companion and an equal."[8]

Speaking about her third husband, Jonathan Fast (thirty to her thirty-six):

"You can imagine the reaction everyone had to our romance. It was as if I were sixty, going with a man of thirty. Actually, even that would be okay, although it wouldn't sit well with many people. The hypocrisy of it! If a woman is six years younger than a man, nobody even bats an eyelash."[9]

And when Gloria Swanson was asked about marrying a

man sixteen years younger, she replied: "A woman, biologically, is not as old as a man. You must remember the menopause; for a woman, this is great! My God, she doesn't have to worry about getting pregnant. She has a sense of freedom, a sense of abandon, which a man has from the beginning."[10]

It is possible that social disapproval of relationships between younger men and older women has been grounded in the fear that the number of child-bearing years would be lessened, diminishing the male's ability to produce children in a monogamous society. In the past, during periods of high infant-mortality rates (due to inadequate hygienic techniques and the absence of proper prenatal care), this taboo served a purpose, but in our present age, with global problems of overpopulation, the argument is no longer viable.

Directly affecting the recent surge of sexual candor and the concomitant search for sexual gratification has been the development of an effective contraceptive, which, in effect, has freed women and allowed them to plan their lives with long-term goals. Technological innovation resulting in greater leisure time (and with actuarial tables projecting a lengthening span of vigorous, healthy life) has spawned a more positive attitude about midlife, which has been confirmed by the proliferation of books and articles on the subject. In addition, the mass-media's exploration (books, television, movies) of various kinds of pairings can only lead to wider sanction of older-woman/younger-man relationships.

The gossip columns have been filled with the news of May-December relationships among the jet set and the Hollywood tinsel crowd. (Princess Margaret, forty-seven, received extensive press on her romance with Roddy Llewellyn, thirty. Jeanne Moreau, forty-nine, married director William Friedkin, thirty-eight. Doris Day married Barry Comden, eleven years younger. Louise Fletcher, forty-four, lives with Morgan Mason, twenty-two. Kim Novak, forty-four, married veterinarian Bob Malloy, thirty-seven. Kate Jackson, twenty-nine, married struggling actor Andrew Stevens, twenty-three.)

Liz Smith, New York *Daily News* columnist, has said: "When men have money and power, they choose younger partners; now it is the same with women."[11]

Until very recently, sexual initiative was always assumed to be the prerogative of the male. We treated the male's sexual precocity as if it were an inherent characteristic. But societal and cultural transformation of mores, plus the birth-control pill, the availability of therapeutic abortion, and the well-documented studies of Masters and Johnson (though all women may not experience orgasm, they are all physiologically capable of having one)[12] and Sherfey, among others, have made strong impacts on society and have helped to change our ingrained patterns of thinking. But today's woman has awakened to the possibility of obtaining the rights historically accorded to men, and with regard to sex, they are more frequently asking themselves the question: If a middle-aged man can be sexually reawakened by a younger woman, doesn't the same principle apply to a middle-aged woman and a younger man?

When economic and social prestige was vested almost exclusively in the male, the qualities valued in the female were most closely a function of her youth: a pretty face, an attractive body, modesty, the potential for bearing many children—attributes that would enhance her husband/lover's image. But society is in a state of flux, and all our stereotypes about relationships are breaking down. Familial and geographic ties are being severed as people feel free, and sometimes compelled, to move in search of economic betterment. And because people are more mobile, the supports they had for old relationships are reduced. Our society has changed to the point where more and more individuals are making their own decisions as to how they want to conduct their lives. And decisions concerning sexual relationships are now being based on feelings, rather than on what is considered the "right" thing to do. Author Nancy Mayer writes: "Mid-life is the time when both sexes become more concerned with pleasing themselves than with placating others."[13]

In a sense, the increase of older-woman/younger-man relationships can be viewed as a reaction against past repressions, as well as a steppingstone to new redefinitions of the bases of sexual attractiveness and emotional maturation. The women that we came to know were accessible—extremely open and willing to share their innermost feelings. The men, on the other hand, wrote long letters of introduction, discussed parts of their relationships on the phone, and told us how eager they were to talk; however, much to our disappointment, only one out of three showed up. When we made follow-up phone calls to reschedule appointments, we learned that the men, who previously were so eager to talk, were no longer so. When we asked them why they had changed their minds, their most frequent comment was: "I guess I just don't want to analyze it." Therefore, if the book appears to deal more with the woman's point of view, that is the reason.

Older Women/Younger Men is not a "how to" guidebook, nor does it advocate these relationships above any other. It simply describes a type of relationship and allows you, the reader, to form your own conclusions. Conventional role models are in the process of shifting. Women and men are beginning to seek out and respond to each other as people. *Older Women/Younger Men* will focus on what might possibly be a new major sociosexual trend.

OLDER WOMEN/
YOUNGER MEN

1

THE PEOPLE INVOLVED

ARE YOU NOW OR HAVE YOU EVER PLAYED A PART IN
AN OLDER-WOMAN/YOUNGER-MAN RELATIONSHIP? IF SO, WE
WOULD LIKE TO TALK WITH YOU FOR A SERIOUS BOOK. CON-
FIDENTIALITY GUARANTEED.

In reply to the above advertisement in newspapers, magazines, and on bulletin boards in universities and adult-educa-
tion centers, hundreds of letters were received from people
who were eager to discuss their relationships. This response
was our first indication of a national trend that crossed social
class and race and that older-woman/younger-man relationships, like other long-held societal taboos, could be discussed openly. The correspondents, people interviewed, and
visual and print media coverage confirmed our feeling that
older-woman/younger-man relationships were increasing and
becoming a more visible alternative life-style.

> I am an older woman who for the last two years has been
> mother, sister, friend and lover to a younger man. May I add
> that it has brought me laughter and tears. . . .
>
> Mary M., forty-three
> Colorado

I've been involved with an older woman since November.
She's forty-six, I'm thirty-five. I can readily understand why

this topic is of interest, having in the last year been exposed to a multiple besetting of emotions and situations.

Jim S.
Florida

Eight months ago I left my husband to be with my lover. I am forty-eight. He is thirty-three. I am happy and satisfied for the first time in my life and would be willing to discuss our relationship with you.

Susan D.
Virginia

I am one of the older women with younger men (44, 24). I not only played a part, but won the starring role and still going strong after four beautiful years.

Arlene W.
Philadelphia

Yes I have! (And there must be thousands like me.) Anyhow, I once attempted to write some of the "adventures" down but first of all I type badly—second, the story is not accurate—in the story I attempted to destroy my boy-lover because he refused me at one point. In real life, it went on for six years until I was too tired of all that vigor. Whatever— you are welcome to the information.

Gail D., thirty-six
Atlanta

I am the younger man (37 to 46) and the last three years have been the happiest ones of my life. You've got to tell people in your book that it's not age that matters, but who, what and where the people are in their *own* stages of development that counts. When you find the person who is right for you, you can't afford to let some dumb number stand in your way. Please feel free to get in touch with us.

Martin P.
Oregon

Hello. I'm twenty-four. I've been living with a thirty-one-year-old woman for the past eight months. I am unsure of my feelings for her and was wondering whether it had anything to do with age. Perhaps if we were to talk, I could better sort out my feelings. Thanks.

Daniel K.
Boston

I was married to a man my own age, had a long-lasting affair with a man thirteen years my senior and am presently having a relationship with a man eleven years my junior. He is the love of my life. For the first time in my life, I feel fulfilled and happy. I'd be very happy to share some of my joy with you and your readers. You may contact me at my office.

Barbara L., thirty-nine
California

Glorious, wonderful, satisfying, fantastic, there aren't enough superlatives to tell you about my marriage to Wendy. It's been three wonderful years. She's forty-nine and I'm thirty-four. We look forward to hearing from you.

Don T.
Minneapolis

I am twenty-two years old, a sophomore in law school. For the past eight months I have been seriously involved with a forty-four-year-old divorcee. The only hitch in our relationship is that she is my mother's best friend. I would be happy to talk to you—with the understanding that confidentiality is a necessity.

Saul W.
New Jersey

I read your ad with great interest. My lover is the same age as my son. It's caused some crazies, some soul-searching, and some re-examination of my values. I'd like to talk with you.

Sharon A., forty-two
California

I'm six months older . . . but he seems ten years older. Do we count? Please let me know.

Carol-Anne S., thirty-three
New York

I am the younger man (27) who had a relationship with an older woman (52) for four years. She was my psychology professor in college. At present it has become difficult to continue due to the fact that I have since graduated and moved to New York while she continues to teach in Vermont. Please call.

Alan R.
New Jersey

Your ad talked directly to me! I am the older woman (35). He is young (24), vibrant and sexy, and has become my confidant and lover. I'd be happy to talk to you.

Sheila Y.
New York

I am twenty-six years old and have had a few short affairs with men aging from seventeen to twenty-one and one deep relationship with a sixteen-year-old. You can call me from 9:30 to 5:30.

Lois W.
Connecticut

I've been working for a terrific woman for the past three years. She is forty-one, I am thirty-one. Nine months ago, we fell in love. Age isn't the problem, the job is, and it becomes more difficult to hide our feelings for each other as the days go by.

Steven N.
Connecticut

I've had affairs with older men and men my own age; the man I'm in love with and married to is five years younger than myself. There was a lot of flak in the beginning—but we've conquered it—and probably grown closer together because of it. The world has joined us, we haven't joined the world.

Madelyn R., thirty
Rhode Island

I've been living with an older woman (28, 40) for the past year. She is not supporting me, nor has she given me a car, clothing or jewelry. And our sex life is more than one big orgasm. I'm really tired of people thinking that just because I'm younger, I'm therefore some kind of gigolo. I'd like to meet with you and try to dispel some myths about this stereotyped relationship.

Howard L.
Boston

If you wish more information concerning older-woman/younger-men relationships possibly I can be of help. I'm financially independent so it gives me time to do as I please. The younger men that I meet attract and hold my attention mainly for sensitivity to their own needs as well as responsiveness to others. I think too many articles of this nature promote the sexual adventure and forget the head spaces and emotional development.

Stephanie (51)
California

Yes I have been involved in a few short and a few long term relationships with older women (Black and white). I'm glad that someone else finds this an important issue. I would be happy to relate my experience.

Peter T., thirty-two
Chicago

Finally a serious book about what seems so perfectly natural to me and the woman I've been living with for the past two years (48 to 56). We say, "It's about time people stopped snickering about a relationship which is perfectly acceptable when the genders are reversed." Talk about the double standard!

Tom H.
Pittsburgh

Author Lance Morrow has written that age has lost its determining relevance as the framework of the sexual drama changes. He says older women are no longer quite so afraid of becoming involved with younger men. With feminism and exposure to the brittle fragility of so many marriages in the seventies, women of almost all ages have developed a certain independence. In the past, as a matter of sociobiological order, desirable women (especially in youth-worshiping America) tended to be those of the courting age, from seventeen or so to about twenty-five or twenty-eight. . . . Girls reaching twenty-five would start to panic about finding a husband, and many, two or three years later, would marry slobs just to change their sexual prefixes.

An entire cathedral of customs and fashions was constructed around the rites of mating, which, especially for women, carried certain age regulations, or at least probabilities. The edifice has by no means been dismantled, but it is greatly altered.[1]

In our own interview with psychotherapist Leah Schaefer another viewpoint was offered: The older woman who is serious about her relationship may be drawn to someone younger as a compensation for her own death concerns. In the back of her mind she might be thinking that if she hangs on to someone young, the youth factor might be contagious. There's the very real possibility of getting a second chance at something.

There are also some women who just "collect" young men. In this case, the older woman may want to play the part of the teacher. It may make her feel powerful. She may feel good about herself because she doesn't have to compete with women her own age, who go with men of a similar age. She may feel more in charge, more in control. And by going from one young man to another, she can avoid the issue of marriage and permanence.

Whatever the internal or external reasons might be, a great number of people are choosing to engage in a pairing that currently goes against the norm. What are the benefits, the pleasures, the joys, the pains, problems, and trouble spots in an older-woman/younger-man relationship? On the following pages, you will meet the people involved in just such pairings, and all of them have their own stories to tell.

Joan, 45; Greg, 24. They dated for over three years and have been married for ten months.

Joan was a petite, compact woman dressed in a gray print polyester pants suit. She had short brown curly hair and blue eyes. Although her only makeup was mascara and lipstick, she seemed to project a glow throughout our interview.

"Greg was living right across the street from me in another apartment house and I never even knew it. One July evening, my next-door neighbor had a heart attack and the police and ambulance arrived at the same time—lights flashing, sirens going . . . big commotion! I ran out with the stretcher and saw Greg standing across the street. He was wearing a pair of cut-off jeans. I remember thinking what a great body he had. My daughter, who turned out to be a year younger than Greg, recognized him and he came over to talk. I liked him immediately. He had a nice way about him and was pleasant and easy to be with. We stood outside, talking, for about an hour. My daughter went out on a date. When I told him that I knew some nice girls to fix him up with, he was agreeable.

"It seems I have a lot of young friends. He took one out and we ran into each other shortly after that. He said she was a 'kid' and that it had been a pleasant evening but nothing special. And then, for the next few months, we kept running into each other—at the supermarket, the drugstore, in the neighborhood bar. Two or three times a week, we'd get together at his place for coffee and talk for a couple of hours; then I'd go home. My husband worked nights, so there was no problem. We would talk about his job: he was working as a construction worker at the time, when he really wanted to go to college; or about my job as a bank teller . . . sometimes about my kids; and later we'd talk about my husband. The amazing thing was that he seemed really interested in listening to me. I mean, he wasn't bored with what I had to say.

"You've got to realize that I've been married to a bastard for twenty-six years, and I knew it wouldn't work from day one. Talk about a dead-end street! I only stayed with him for the sake of my three kids. He was just no good and he often became violent. He once blackened my eye so badly that I was out of work for a week. If you didn't keep your head, you'd be lost. Then, when he'd drink, he'd look back over the years, kind of reminisce about his life. Over and over and over again, he'd talk about all the good deals that got away. He was two years older than me, going on eighty. As my kids grew older, they knew the situation, they knew our marriage was bad. There was no communication, no talk. I was the mother and the father; my husband was someone who just took up space.

"I think that when I turned thirty-seven I started worrying about what I was going to do with my life. I certainly wasn't happy. I was an overweight, middle-aged housewife, in a rut. I don't think I felt bitter. I just felt like I was biding my time. Anyway, I started going out to dinner with men friends from work. No sex; just company. I began to go away on vacations by myself or with a girlfriend. About five years ago, my kids started taking me to discothèques. I love to dance and had a ball. A lot of the men in the discos were much younger than I was. They came on pretty strong. I think they take friendship the wrong way. I was never on the make. They were. You can't imagine the attention I got: men were flirting with me; they were finding me attractive. And there were times when I liked it. . . . I certainly wasn't being flattered at home.

"One night, I ran into Greg on the street and he suggested we go out on a real date. You know . . . drinks, dinner, and dancing. I was kind of pleased but didn't want him to spend his money on me. But, three nights later, we went out. We started off in a bar. It was quite crowded and we kept bumping into each other. Suddenly it was all there: the bells, the firecrackers, the desire. I used to read about that in books, but I never thought it would happen to me. We left the bar and drove straight to a motel. Well, it was a disaster! We were both too anxious; too nervous and very embarrassed. We laugh about it today. Later that week, we tried again and it was great! My sex life with my husband was . . . well, forget it . . . no, I was used, like the old 'Saturday-night-is-bath-night' routine.

"About a month later, Greg decided to move. He wanted to be out of *my* neighborhood, he said. He asked me to run away with him and I laughed. I jokingly said that in three years' time, when my youngest would be eighteen and out of the house, then if it was still right for the both of us, I'd do it.

"I helped him fix up his new apartment, and we just kept getting closer. And it wasn't just sex—although that was pretty fantastic. I got to know his every mood, all his likes and dislikes. And he knew me, inside out. We'd sit and talk for hours. Sometimes I'd get hung up—I'd feel like I was his mother—and want to break it off. But he'd just laugh and say I was foolish. I purposely stayed away on weekends—for two and a half years. I felt this was his time to do whatever he wanted to do without anyone looking over his shoulder. I knew he dated a lot. He told me he was going out. But there was never a lasting, serious relationship, never anything permanent.

"So after a great deal of talk, Greg and I decided to go away for a week. My husband was used to me taking a separate vacation. And, as long as he had his TV dinners, he would probably never miss me. The night before the trip, I had a bad case of jitters. The thought of spending twenty-four hours a day together scared the hell out of me. But this was going to be it for us; it would either make us or break us. We became closer. Everything just seemed to work out right. We sat in the sun, walked along the beach, and went sight-seeing and shopping in the market. We went to nightclubs, danced, and had fantastic dinners. And something more important: we were able to be quiet with each other.

"About a month after we came home, Greg got sick. My doctor suggested surgery. I was there every single night. It was work, hospital, home, for two straight weeks. Although the operation wasn't serious, I was petrified, thinking I might lose him. I guess that was when it really hit home how much I loved him.

"I wanted him to go to college, if that was his dream. If we were to have any kind of future, I didn't want him to have any regrets. We talked about it for months, and the best deal was the service. So he went into the Army. When he walked through the gates of the camp, my heart dropped to my knees. I was sure it would be over for us. There would be guys his own age, he'd want to run around, or he'd find someone else to love. But he called every other day and I called him on weekends. My telphone bill was enormous. Then I went to visit him for a week. At first, I felt very self-conscious at the base. We went to the club, and I felt like I was at a prom. He introduced me to everyone as his 'girl,' and that made me feel proud. We danced a lot, joked and fooled around with the other couples, and by the end of the evening I felt accepted. I surprised myself by having such a good time that I stayed two weeks!

"The day after I got home, he called and asked me to marry him. Here I had already decided to live with him, and he wanted to marry me! The next day, I took a loan. At four that morning, I moved out of my house and into a hotel. That day, I filed for divorce.

"I think when you really care about a person, you keep things quiet and . . . wait. We waited for three years. My kids were probably the most surprised, because they never knew things had gotten so serious. They just saw Greg as a friend. They all get along real well. My son's reaction was: 'He must really love you, because you don't have a dime.'

"I wondered if his friends would say: 'What's the matter, you can't get a young chick?' Then we talked about it and decided that if people wanted to talk, they would. As I've said, I've always had young friends and I guess we sort of blend in. People either accept us or not—not because of age but because of who we are.

"I was worried because I can't have more children. I pointed this out to him but he said it didn't matter and that we could always adopt. I was agreeable to that.

"Greg has changed a lot over the years. He left home when he was sixteen and didn't get in touch with his family until three years ago. I insisted that he talk to his folks. He found that time had changed them also, and began going there for Sunday dinner. They don't know about me, and I really wouldn't want to face his mother. She's a year older than I am, and from everything he's told me, she just wouldn't understand about us. He wants to tell her, but I say no. It's enough for me that they finally care about their son. If Greg's content, then I am too.

"When we're walking down the street or eating in a restaurant or making love, we don't talk about age, we talk about life."

Hector, 23; Rita, 39. Hector dated Rita for four months before moving in with her. Rita has an eight-year-old son from a previous marriage.

We met Hector in a coffee shop in midafternoon. Tall and dark, with black wavy hair, he was dressed in a denim suit, pale blue shirt, and cowboy boots. He had an infectious grin and was enormously appealing.

"At the time I met Rita, I was working as a messenger, a summer job that I took after graduating from college. She signed for the package I delivered to her office. It was a scorching hot day and she looked unbelievably cool and beautiful. I still remember the color of her dress: a rich green that reminded me of new grass. I was at her office numerous times over the summer and, each time, we talked a little more. I started looking forward to seeing her and even tried to trade off with the other messengers for packages to take to her office building. One day, I brought her some iced tea; another time, it was a single rose. A supposedly five-minute visit was stretched to fifteen minutes, then to thirty-five. I finally got up enough nerve to ask her out for lunch, and she said yes.

"I'm Puerto Rican and the youngest of six children, all girls. We have a very close family. Three of my sisters have married but still live within a two-block radius of my mother's home. My father died ten years ago, so I just remember growing up surrounded by women. I guess I was pretty spoiled, being the youngest and the only boy.

"I was the only one in the family to go to college. I went on a scholarship and lived at home. My family was so proud; each of the girls contributed part of their salary checks so I'd have the right clothes to wear. When I came home, after my part-time job, I'd stay up late studying at the kitchen table. My mother would walk around shushing the girls. I can still hear her saying, 'Sh. . . , sh. . . , Hector's studying.' She'd always have a big pot of coffee on the stove for me and a sandwich or a dessert tucked away under a napkin. Education has always been important to my mother. It was a way out of the *barrio*. She thought you could be anything if you went to college. When I graduated, the whole family attended the ceremony, dressed in their best. We had a big party at home where half the neighborhood came and brought food and ate, drank, and danced all night.

"Rita and I went to lunch many times. She was divorced and lived in an apartment in Forest Hills with her eight-year-old son. I went out one Saturday and spent the day with them. It was a delight. Her son, Mark, and I hit it off immediately. I think I spent more time with him than I did with Rita. We played ball, went to the park, had pizza. He was yawning by the time I got him home. I felt . . . close to him. His father hadn't been around for five years, and I think he missed some male company. I guess I kinda identified with him. Don't get me wrong. Rita is a great mother, but there needs to be a male-female balance for a young kid. Someone to do 'man's things' with. God, I should know!

"When the summer ended, I entered a computer-programming course. I continued to see Rita in the evenings and on weekends but still lived at home. My sisters would bring around their friends or give me phone numbers to call—but I wasn't interested.

"I was spending more and more time with Rita and little Mark and started staying overnight. I enjoyed being there. It was cozy. We were like a family, except some of the roles got reversed. I usually got home in the afternoon and picked Mark up from school. We'd go to the park for a while and then shop for groceries in the supermarket. I learned how to cook from my mother and was pretty good. I'd prepare dinner, Mark would set the table, and everything would be ready when Rita got home. She and I would do the dishes while Mark did his homework. We'd all watch TV, and then Mark would go to bed. He insisted that we both tuck him in, and then Rita would read to him until he fell asleep.

"Rita is sixteen years older than me, but I didn't fall in love with her age, I fell in love with her. Perhaps I was naturally comfortable with her since I'd grown up with older women. She was soft and gentle and, I felt, very vulnerable. I wanted to protect her, to take care of her, to make her life better if I could.

"Rita is a small, good-looking redhead. Her parents got divorced when she was eleven. Her mother, who had a drinking problem, had a steady procession of 'uncles' drifting in and out of their house. When Rita was sixteen, she ran away from home. She took a series of jobs, married at eighteen, divorced at twenty-four, married again at twenty-eight, and divorced once more at thirty-two. She is at the same time a child and a woman. She's been terribly supportive of me. She inspires me to be 'more,' to go for bigger and better things. She's a good listener and is eager to hear about what I'm learning in school.

"When I moved in with Rita, two months ago, my family was very upset. My mother kept crying and wringing her hands. She called my married sisters to come over and talk to me. It was not only that Rita was older but that she was white, divorced, and had a child. I was doing everything that was unacceptable. They wanted me to settle down with some nice, eligible Puerto Rican girl. They didn't understand about attraction or about love—well they did, but only if it were with another Puerto Rican. I had very mixed feelings the night I packed up my things. I was torn between Rita and my family—and Rita won out. I still feel very uneasy when I go there, once a week, for dinner. They're all very polite, but it's not like it was. Maybe, in time. . . .

"Sex with Rita is dynamite. I wasn't a virgin, but I didn't have that much experience. She has been guide and teacher. She's not afraid to initiate sex, and it's nice not to always have to be the aggressor.

"Rita and I laugh a lot together, over silly things, over nothing. She said she feels there's joy in her house for the first time, something she'd been missing. She calls me a natural father and is pleased when Mark and I go out for the day to do 'manly' things.

"There are times when Rita is concerned about her age.

She'll spend a lot of time in the bathroom looking at herself. Sometimes she'll stand nude in front of the mirror, examining her body. When we first made love, she was embarrassed by an old appendectomy scar. She needs constant reassurance that she looks good. She spends a lot of time shopping, and I think she has great taste. Yet, when she models all the clothing at home, if I don't say how great this one is or that one looks, then she'll take it back first thing in the morning. I'd like her to be more self-confident, but perhaps she needs time to know that she's really loved and that I'm not going to walk out on her.

"I love Rita. I've already given up my place in my family for her. If things continue the way they've been going, I'd like to marry her, if she'd have me, when I finish my schooling. I love Mark and would adopt him, and I'm hoping that Rita and I would be able to have a child of our own one day."

Penny, 36; Len, 28. Penny preferred to spend a large part of the interview discussing her predilection for younger men. She considered her affair with Len to be a serious one, to the point where she was thinking of marriage.

Penny was a petite five feet. Even with her three-inch-heeled shoes, she seemed vulnerable and in need of protection. Her gamine appearance was accentuated by her pixie-styled jet black hair. Her green eyes matched the green-and-white-checked designer dress she wore with some fragile-looking pieces of gold jewelry.

"I don't think I made a conscious decision to only date younger men . . . at least not in the beginning. It just seemed to work out that way.

"In my senior year of college I began seeing a fellow student in my English honors class. I didn't know that he had advanced placement in this one subject and that he was really a sophomore. When I did find out, after three dates, I stopped seeing him. It was too bad, 'cause he was a really nice guy. I liked him, but I was still caught up in the American myth that said the man *should* be older, or at least your own age!

"During the next five years, I pretty much followed tradition. All my affairs were with older men.

"When I was twenty-six, I fell head over heels in love with Paul. We met on a ski weekend and spent the next six months in each other's pocket. He was twenty-two and I didn't give a damn! Age meant nothing—Paul meant everything. We broke up because we both felt we needed more space—more time to find ourselves.

"In the next four years, I just seemed to attract younger men. I sometimes felt like I was wearing a sign saying: 'Only younger men need apply.' I met them on the tennis court, in the discos, at my neighborhood bar. And when I was in need of rescuing; like hanging pictures, or carrying groceries, well, they always seemed to be the ones who came to my aid.

"I've always looked young. And my size probably adds to that impression. I was a tomboy. I loved sports and always played and got along well with my two younger brothers and their friends. I think I'm a good pal—I'm caring and supportive. I've always liked men and have had an easy time talking to them, being their friend.

"I was thirty-six last week, and lately there've been moments when I've worried about aging. My two younger brothers are married. One even has a child. I think my parents are disappointed that I haven't gotten married . . . but they're smart enough not to mention the subject in my presence. I'd like to have children—so you never can tell. Oh, I was telling you about feeling old, no, older. Well, you can see I have a few gray hairs and I've noticed some wrinkles around my eyes. Luckily, my figure's in good shape. I run three miles every day and play tennis twice a week. But the real beauty secret may be that I'm involved with a new man. Have been for the past four months, and this one could be it!

"Of course he's younger. Eight years, to be exact. My parents know I'm seeing someone and they're happy. They don't know about the age difference. They know I like younger men and I think they're ashamed of that. It's like their daughter has a social disease called 'rob the cradle.' They've asked me why I don't go out with men a few years older. Well, they're fuddy-duddies. The men I know that are in their forties are not terribly appealing. They don't know how to dance and think smoking a joint will lead to heroin addiction. They won't stay up all night. They're not into just having fun over nothing. They're so serious, everything has got to have a meaning. They're all having their mid-life crisis and falling apart over it. And the sex is nothing to brag about. For the most part, their bodies are unattractive. Most of them have sat behind a desk too long. They don't give a damn about muscle tone and so they've let themselves go. They've had too many expense-account lunches with too many martinis.

"I said I liked men and I do; I enjoy their company. I don't want to battle for supremacy; and I neither want to be dominant nor subservient. I want to be equal . . . and for some reason I find this equality with younger men. Maybe it's the age, innocence or naïveté—whatever. With younger men you don't have power games or ego-tripping.

"I don't give a damn what society or my parents say. My goal is to be happy and if a younger man is the instrument of my happiness, well, then, it's no one's business but my own.

"I look at single women my age and older and feel sorry for them. Because of conditioning, they've ruled out half the male population as a source for potential dates and mates. If these women want to bitch about available men it's strictly in their heads. They can buck the corporate powers that be for equal opportunity, yet still have this incredible mind-set when it comes to men.

"I'm an account executive at a large advertising agency and I met Len when I was doing a presentation for his company. We worked closely over our joint project, usually having a relaxing, wind-down late dinner. I not only was attracted to him—he's very good-looking—but I liked him also. We found that we worked well together, that our interests meshed perfectly. When he talked business, I knew what he meant, and vice versa. And, surprise! He was a runner too. We're both very health conscious and haven't eaten red meat in the last month. He spends four nights at my apartment, the rest of the week I'm at his.

"Eight years at this point is a snap of the fingers. It doesn't mean a thing. The age difference has evaporated. Physically, socially, career-wise . . . we're equal.

"And as I've gotten older, I've changed my view of sex. It used to be important for me to sleep with every man I met, to see what kind of lover he would be. And young men—I must have had a hundred of them—were the greatest. But I felt like the keeper of the score card. Was he gentle? Was there arousing foreplay? Could he keep an erection? Did he wait for me to come or was he merely interested in his own orgasm? No tabulation of feelings—just a tally of how good he was. Now, sex is just one aspect of a relationship; it means something, but it doesn't mean everything. Len and I enjoy sex and it's good and it has nothing to do with age. It has to do with the fact that we care about each other.

"I'm not terribly surprised that I'm involved with a younger man to the point where I could consider marrying Len. I guess, if something works out well—my liking for—and getting along with younger men—then, sure I'd continue this same pattern, up to and including marriage. It seems only logical."

Our interview was completed when Penny turned at the door and added: "The question shouldn't be: 'Why a younger man?' but 'Why *not* a younger man?' "

Barbara, 44; Gary, 23. They have been living together for two years.

Barbara was a petite natural redhead. She had fair skin, blue eyes, a sprinkling of freckles across her nose. She was dressed in tight chocolate-brown leather pants and a beige silk shirt. She wore gold earrings, chains, and bracelets, the sounds of which punctuated her enthusiastic conversation.

"Gary and I met in a discothèque. I was there with some friends and I pointed him out to one of the women while commenting that he reminded me of a man I was dating. During the evening, he asked me to dance. I couldn't help noticing how well we moved together. I thought he was older because of his beard, and later he said that he thought I was a lot younger. I guess we both made an age mistake based on looks. I gave him my number, because he said he might know a contact for my business; I design and sell my own jewelry.

"I wasn't looking to get involved—with anyone. I had been divorced eight months, my jewelry business was taking off, I was seeing lots of men, and had my own darling apartment. I was really feeling liberated. And would you believe, a week and a half later he moved in.

"This is how it happened. He called the day after we went to the disco and we went out the following three nights in a row: dancing, movies, to Chinatown. All this time, he had been living with his uncle in Queens, who kept hounding him to 'get straight' as he called it. You know, cut his beard, dress more conventionally—which meant wear a tie and a jacket. The funny thing was, he was dressed up for the three nights that we went out—in the *same* suit, shirt, and tie. Finally, he asked if he could come over and take a shower. At this point, I wasn't looking for a roommate; I was just feeling awfully sorry for him. Hmmm, on second thought, maybe I was. Anyway, we never got out that night—and we spent the next few days in the apartment—eating, sleeping, talking, and making love. We found we had a lot of things in common. I still felt sorry for him and told him I'd go to Queens to meet his uncle. When we got there, everything Gary owned was boxed up and waiting for him. He had been kicked out, and his uncle never even said a word. That night, he moved in with me, but it was only going to be *temporary*. I laugh because now it has been a little over two years! He was the original man who came to shower.

"His business was a blind. He really wanted to be an actor but has had difficulty getting parts. He's been driving a cab nights for the past sixteen months. Since I free-lance, we spend a lot of time together because our schedules are so open. We've settled down to a nice, comfortable pattern. He's warm, affectionate, companionable, easy to be with. He even shops in the supermarket . . . something my ex wouldn't be caught dead doing. We share almost everything.

"In the beginning I know that I felt very self-conscious walking down the street with him. He said he felt proud having me on his arm. It was strange. I kept trying to keep my head, with that 'old' number buried in it, separated from the good feelings in my heart. I know I look young. I've always kept myself in good condition. I felt like two people: the chronological me and the real me.

"I left my ex with a great deal of bitterness. I had been your typical suburban housewife dabbling in good works. My only delight in the last ten years came through my art classes, where I learned to make jewelry. My husband had been drinking heavily on and off for years. A lot of times, he was out of control and abusive. The man had a really foul mouth. Things got so bad that we once went for a whole month without talking to each other. Maybe it was the women's movement that gave me the final push. I had been doing a lot of reading, you know, all those books and magazine articles and some deep soul-searching, and I felt there had to be something more for me in life. I asked myself how long was I willing to stay in a dead-end relationship? I went to a lawyer and explained my situation. I left the following day. My daughter was finishing college in another state. I knew she'd be okay. But I felt guilty about my son, who is now seventeen. I felt like I deserted him when he should have had a mother. But, in my new life, I just couldn't take him with me. Now he seems to understand my rationale, but for a while there it was pretty rough going.

"Gary is a few months older than my daughter. That's wild! The four of us have become very close. The two of them sometimes come and spend weekends with us. We smoke pot together, go dancing, just enjoy each other's vibes. My children think we make a very hip couple, and that pleases me tremendously.

"I've never met any of Gary's friends. He was an orphan, adopted at five by a very wealthy Boston couple who shuffled him in and out of boarding schools. For all the time they spent with him, I can't quite understand why they wanted a child. He bummed around the country for a couple of years and wound up with his uncle (who never really accepted him) after he ran out of money in New York.

"Our friends are creative, arty people. They don't really move in the straight, conservative business world. They're people who are breaking in as painters, writers, and actors. And they all accept him. In our social world, age really isn't considered that important. I sometimes go out with men my own age whom I meet through my work, but there's never sex. Men my age can take me to places that Gary can't afford. For instance, he'd never be able to spring for a fifty-dollar dinner. It's a turn-on sometimes, and Gary understands. Yet, if he began going out, which he doesn't at this time, I'd be insanely jealous and probably wouldn't speak to him for days.

"Look, this is the end, not the means to an end. I know this relationship can't last. There will come a point when it's time to move on, for both of us. At the moment, I feel like I'm a good training ground for him. I've taught him how to cook, clean, fix things around the apartment. He's become a fantastically adept, considerate lover. Someday he'll make someone a good husband. Meanwhile, I never forget that I'm the one who has the power. It's my apartment and I have the option to throw him out—anytime I want.

"Back to age. I've always stayed in good shape. I'm proud

of my body. I've always been physically active, into sports. I dress young. I feel young about myself. But . . . two nights ago we had a big argument and I said to him: 'You're using up all my good years. When you leave, I'll be a shriveled-up old shell and no one will want me.' I guess I'm beginning to feel restless. There are moments when I feel I've lost my independence, and that worries me. I feel more married now than before. Hell, it's going to end.

"I've tried to get him out four times, but he stays . . . and I let him. One day soon, though, it's going to be over."

Diane, 36; *Joe*, 24. Diane and Joe had an affair that lasted eight months. Diane felt her relationship helped save her marriage of eleven years.

Diane was a pretty, soft-looking woman. She had a full face, framed by loosely waved shiny brown hair, and blue-gray eyes. She was dressed in navy cotton slacks, a red-white-and-blue long-sleeved tee shirt, and navy espadrilles. She carried a large straw handbag and looked every inch the contented suburban matron.

"I've been married for eleven years. I met Larry in college and it was love at first sight. We were both sophomores at the time. We lost our virginity to each other in the beginning of our junior year. The day after we graduated, my parents gave us a grand, showy white wedding which is still the talk of the family.

"Larry is an accountant. I taught art in elementary school for two years. We lived in a one-bedroom apartment on the upper East Side for three years and then moved to a four-bedroom house in Bayside after Jennie was born. Two years later, I had Mike.

"Larry and I have a good, solid marriage . . . now. A few years ago, I couldn't have said that. And five months ago, I wouldn't have imagined sharing what changed our lives—with anyone. Yet, if my involvement with Joe helped me and my marriage, then maybe it's worth telling other people about.

"There I was, very average, middle-class, one child in kindergarten, the other in second grade, a station wagon in the garage, and a husband who came home every night on the six-nineteen.

"I never really enjoyed the sexual act, but I'm a good actress and I assumed our sexual life was satisfactory. He never complained. But what did I know? Larry was my one and only lover. I read magazine articles, took those self-scoring tests, and we seemed to be in good marital shape. Perhaps our sex life wasn't absolutely constant over the years. The kids took a lot of effort; Mike was a very sickly baby. I think I saw the pediatrician those first few years as often as I saw my best friend. I felt knee-deep in dirty diapers, strained vegetables, and pull toys. All day long I'd be saying 'No, no, no.' And finally, when I'd be ready to collapse for the night, I'd be saying those exact same words to Larry.

"Tax time has always been the hardest part of the year for us. Larry has loads of clients, and they always file their returns at the last minute. Because of the incredible work load, he'd often miss the last train and stay over in the city. I got used to it over the years and just pretended he was away on a business trip. Two years ago, though, I found myself playing the game, but with a new set of rules, none of which I had agreed to.

"This time, there was nothing last-minute or casual involved. He packed a bag and announced that he'd made a reservation at a small mid-town hotel. It seemed logical at the time. He was planning ahead and I only felt compassion that he was working so hard. When he left on Monday morning he said he'd be back on Saturday. I was surprised at the length of time he'd be staying in the city, but no little bell went off to make me uneasy or suspicious. Larry called the first three nights complaining of his work load and I felt sorry for him.

"I called him on Thursday at the office—to sort of cheer

him up—and was told by his secretary that he'd left at noon. I was surprised and immediately called the hotel, thinking he was ill. The desk clerk said he hadn't seen him come in but that Mrs. _____ was in the room and should he ring? I hung up, stunned, and just sat at the kitchen table until the kids came home from their afterschool center. That whole evening passed in a daze. I did things automatically, my mind placed on 'hold' until I could go to bed.

"And then I cried, on the freshly ironed yellow-flowered sheets. The tears were for me and the kids, for Larry, and for what I had thought was a good marriage.

"The next day was a blur. I got through it, but I don't remember anything except crying myself to sleep.

"Larry came home Saturday afternoon and I had to bite my tongue to keep from accusing him in front of the children. Finally they went to bed, and the minute I shut their door and went back downstairs I started crying. I just couldn't stop. I think Larry was shocked. He didn't know what was going on. He came over to me and held out his arms. I said, 'No,' and waved him away. He stood and watched me hugging myself and crying. Finally the storm passed, and we walked into the den, where I collapsed into an armchair.

"We talked until three-thirty in the morning. He acknowledged the affair and said there had been a few other women over the years. We talked honestly and openly—not about grocery bills or the gardening . . . but about what had happened to us, our goals, when I wanted to be an artist, about our life in suburbia and how it had soured right along with the crab grass.

"Don't get me wrong; everything wasn't immediately blissful. I needed time to put things in perspective, to face the hurt and put it behind me. And I think that Larry and I were determined to make things work in a new way.

"A few months later, I enrolled in an art class at our adult education center. I hadn't sketched in years and was very nervous. I arrived early and started talking to the man next to me—a graduate student at our local college. After class we went out for coffee. We did this for the next four sessions. Joe was so comfortable to be with and so easy to talk to. I enjoyed being with him and anxiously looked forward to each week's class. I was feeling brighter about my life and happy for the first time in months. Larry and I were getting along better, the kids were thriving, and I was painting.

"Joe asked me to lunch and I went, all dressed up, like for a date. I had two glasses of wine and was feeling young and giggly. He put his hand over mine and I loved it. I was feeling attractive and desirable. He was twenty-four, blond and good-looking, the athletic type, and the complete opposite of Larry, who was slight and dark. We agreed to meet again the next week and I was aglow with anticipation. I think I wanted something to happen, yet was afraid to acknowledge the feeling. Maybe I wanted some kind of revenge, maybe I was turned on by Joe. I'm not sure which feeling was more accurate.

"I met Joe for lunch and it was very romantic. He told me he couldn't get me out of his mind. That he thought I was funny and clever, and very appealing. That he wanted to make love to me. I felt high as a kite, as if I could fly without wings. I was young and carefree and beautiful. We went to a large hotel out by the airport and it was there I began to get nervous. Joe signed in for us and I joined him in the room, where he was in the process of taking off his clothes. I just stood there and stared. He was wearing navy jockey shorts. Larry always wore white boxer trunks. And then he was naked. The only man I had seen outside of my husband. Joe looked at me and smiled. I started to tremble. He took me in his arms and held me. My heart was beating so fast I was afraid I was going to pass out. He led me to the bed and slowly helped me undress. I remember holding my stomach in, glad that I was wearing a lacy new bra. He was already hard and his penis looked huge. I was wet by that time and he slid into me quite easily.

"My affair with Joe lasted for eight months. There was never any question of love. We were friends and fellow artists. Joe taught me that sex could be fun. We made it on the floor, in the shower, on the grass at a local park, and in the car. There were times when I felt extremely paranoid. Loyal, faithful mother, president of the PTA, and sex slave to a man over ten years my junior. When I went to him at our different meeting places, I felt like a spy—disguised with my collar pulled up, a large hat covering my hair, and a huge pair of sunglasses. Then I'd run home all sticky from making love to serve SpaghettiO's and help the children with their school work.

"Larry found me more relaxed, more sensitive to his moods, and more ready to try different things in bed. He never even questioned my new outlook; just commented that I seemed somehow happier, more content with life in general. He was proud of my paintings, and thought that returning to my art was the key.

"Joe and I are no longer lovers, but we are still friends. He'll be getting married in a few months and I couldn't be happier for him. I think that because of his age he was a far more tender, more considerate person than someone older— who had been around and perhaps become jaded. While we were together I never felt old. The years just peeled away and I felt rejuvenated.

"I am back to being faithful wife and have no desire to stray. Larry and I went on a second honeymoon a while back and it was sensational. I love him very much and see no reason to tell him about Joe. We have a totally new relationship now, and it's a special one that I know we'll work very hard to maintain.

"I recently read that Dr. Joyce Brothers, whom I consider to be so very straight and moral, had changed her attitude toward infidelity. Now she believes an affair can boost a woman's confidence, just as it did mine, and in many cases can enhance a marriage. I couldn't agree more."

Julia, 25; Evan, 16. Their relationship lasted for the duration of a three-month summer vacation, which they spent living together in Berkeley, California. Presently, they are friends.

Julia was approximately five feet four inches tall, heavily made up, her unruly brown hair reached half way down her back. She wore tight navy slacks and an open silk shirt that displayed her ripe full figure. She was currently employed as a saleslady in a boutique in New York, her fifth such position.

"I met Evan on a Sunday afternoon in Central Park. He was sitting on the grass reading a paperback book. I approached him and asked if he liked the story, a science-fiction novel I had already read. We talked for the whole afternoon, went to Nathan's for hot dogs, and walked around the city. He looked young . . . but sixteen? Anyway, he told me he had no place to stay. He had arrived from Chicago by bus earlier that morning and was going to call relatives. But we had talked away the day and it was now one in the morning. I told him he could stay at my place. We slept together but there was no sex. He wore his underwear to bed and fell asleep immediately. I stayed awake and looked at him. He was beautiful. About six feet tall, tan, blond hair. And his body: good build, muscular, long lean legs, a beauty mark on the outside of his left thigh . . . gorgeous! Although I wanted him as a sexual partner, I was determined not to make the advance, not to be the seducer. I didn't want to be some 'dirty old lady.'

"He stayed with me for the following week. I worked during the day, he explored New York. At night, we talked, went to movies, and watched television together. When we went to sleep the fourth night, he began caressing me, and that was my 'go' signal. We made love. He was hardly 'experienced,' but he wasn't a virgin. I snuggled in his arms all that night as we talked and dozed and made love again. He convinced me at five in the morning to quit my job and go to California with him. Wait, this wasn't as big a deal as you might think. I was a salesgirl heading nowhere. I had no ties or responsibilities. So why not California? In the morning, he called his mother and told her he was traveling west with a friend. She agreed to send him money for the trip. I quit my job that day and arranged to sublet my apartment the following week. We spent the remaining time giggling and getting ready for our big adventure.

"My father is a well-known lawyer. I saw him before I left and told him of our plans. He said that when he was younger he went with a much older woman and that it was a very valuable experience. He thought I'd be good for Evan. I think I've always respected my father's opinion, even though we've been through some rough family times. My parents divorced after twenty-seven years and my father married someone twenty-five years younger. To say I was surprised would be a gross understatement. I get along with her now, but at first I just stayed away from the house. I couldn't understand why she married my father. Who knows . . . maybe she really does love him. Anyway, my mother was unprepared for the divorce. She's alone now with a crappy job and no social life. I think she's frigid, hardened on men. She constantly tells me: 'Don't give in. Don't always say yes!' Now I feel closer to my aunt than I do to her. And I have a younger sister I haven't talked to in two years. We had a rather violent disagreement about the men we were seeing. So we decided not to speak. I guess my family background isn't too stable.

"Evan is an only child. He has been pretty much on his own. His mother sounds like a social dynamo. She's either giving parties or taking trips to Europe. She just divorced her fourth husband, and she's only forty-one! Evan talks more about his housekeeper (some nice old grandmother type) than he does about his mother. Freaky, huh?

"We went to Berkeley and had a fantastic summer. I supported him but not extravagantly . . . just bought food and stuff. And I used my Master Charge when we felt like living it up. When my money ran out, we both got jobs. I became a waitress; Evan got a job doing construction on a new library. We worked for a month and then quit and lived on the money we had made.

"A day that stands out in my mind was when I hurt my ankle and Evan took me to the hospital. He was so considerate, so caring, so worried about me. I was really touched by his concern. I had to stay off my foot for two days, and he brought me flowers, candy, and magazines. I'm a sucker for that kind of attention.

"Oh, and he was tremendously anxious about the possibility of me getting pregnant. He kept saying to me: 'You're sure you're not going to get pregnant? Are you absolutely positive that your coil works?' My God, if there was one thing I was totally certain about, it was that I'd never make a sixteen-year-old a father!

"I developed early and was always self-conscious about being so busty. At seventeen, I had my first affair. I've had a hell of a lot of one-night stands. I've been in a lot of bad relationships, I guess through my own fault. I lived with a guy for two years. He was four years younger than I am, and he was the worst. A baby. Evan is different, probably because he was never treated like a child. There was no mother in constant attendance and his real father died when he was young. He grew up early, because he had to. Everyone who meets Evan, likes him. He was my joy pill. For the whole time we were together, I was never once depressed. I was always happy, always on a continual high.

"I think young men are freer in spirit than the older ones. They just don't think about serious things. Life is a lark to them, and everything is always fine. How nice it is to share their world: free of responsibility, free of worry. I got great pleasure doing things for Evan. I did his laundry, cooked his meals, helped him choose some new clothes. I liked being his teacher. I liked being in charge and taking care of him. But there were also many times when I was on his level. We were really like two kids for most of last summer. I remember a day when I braided his hair and he braided mine. Corny? No, fun! And we seemed to be always laughing together, always having a good time.

"I think I've always been attracted to young guys. Males my own age are so messed up; they're more concerned with themselves than with me. I think I spent time with these guys (same age or older) as an ego booster. They would say: 'Tell me how great I am,' and I would oblige. That was my function. Maybe I feel threatened by men my own age. They seem to be in competition with me or are always testing. With younger men I think I come off as an impressive woman. . . . I'm experienced, I've been around. That's not the way I appear to men my age. And I don't go out any more with older guys; I'm just not after anyone's money.

"The summer passed too quickly. The night before he flew back to Chicago, we went out and celebrated. My treat, of course. Then we made love all night. He always enjoyed it and was ready to do or try anything. One day, he came home with four sex manuals, and we tried every damn position there was. For the next few days, I was so sore I couldn't walk. Oh, and let me tell you about the food games. I had honey on one arm, chocolate syrup on the other and whipped cream down my middle. I guess I don't have to explain the rules . . . you can guess.

"At the airport the next morning, I started crying and couldn't stop. I felt like someone had died . . . maybe some part of me.

"We've been in contact this year, but not regularly. I'm sure, though, that he'll be in New York for the summer, and then we'll see what happens. I realize that he's been dating and that because of his age he's not emotionally ready to get involved with one woman. I think that a woman in this kind of a relationship has got to understand that being with a younger man is only for a temporary period of time.

"Because of my good feelings about Evan, I have consciously looked for much younger men this year. The ones I've found have been pretty poor. They sleep with you so they can tell their friends. That's all they want. I guess a lot of them are still kids. I don't see myself getting married. I can't see staying with someone so long and remaining happy. I'm afraid I'd get bored and then I'd become bitter. I've thought about having children. I want them someday and it wouldn't matter if I wasn't married.

"My summer with Evan was the high point of my life. I have never loved anyone like I loved him. Now I'll just wait and see what happens."

Kendra, 49; Phil, 37. They have been having an affair for eight months.

Kendra was a stunning brunette whose age was not readily apparent. She had just returned from playing tennis. She wore a white dress with green accents that perfectly matched her eyes. The simple tennis outfit showed off her deep tan and trim size-eight figure to their best advantage.

"I met Phil early one Sunday morning in the park. We were both waiting to use the tennis courts.

"I'm an attractive woman, and at forty-nine I feel like the commercial that says: 'You're not getting older, you're getting better.' Phil and I were physically attracted to each other from the beginning. I thought he looked somewhere around my age. He's tall and nice-looking. Age, though, has never been my hang-up; it's height. I just don't like short men! Phil towered over my five-foot-five frame. With his beard and twinkly eyes he reminded me of a jolly Teddy bear.

"We had a long wait ahead of us and we seemed to immediately delve into each other's personal life without all that bar-talk trivia. He found out that I was a widow of six years, that I had two children in college, that I worked two days a week in an art gallery. I learned that he was a divorced stockbroker with no children, had two museum memberships, and played the piano. We both found to our increasing pleasure that we loved Chinese food, spy stories, Groucho Marx, classical music, and almost any sport played outdoors. And that we disliked punk rock, rude children, creamy desserts, and rainy days.

"He had a good sense of humor, and it was terribly refreshing to laugh so early in the morning.

"When I asked him for his phone number, he smiled when giving it to me, then added: 'I like you. Call me.' Turnabout, fair play, right?

"I called him ten days later, and when he heard my voice, the first thing he said was 'What took you so long?'

"We've been seeing each other for the past eight months. It's a comfortable, easygoing relationship. We go to the theater a lot, have dinner out three or four nights a week, and play tennis twice a week. I'd say we spend about five nights a week in each other's company.

"I see nothing strange in our relationship. It's the other people, the ones locked into their own tight, narrow-minded, frightened worlds, that find something dirty or unhealthy when the couple consists of an older woman and a younger man.

"A man can date a woman his daughter's age and we don't bat an eye. Last week, my twenty-one-year-old niece married a man of forty-three. They said she'd made a 'good match.' But when I go around with someone twelve years my junior, my relatives fear for my sanity. They call it 'middle-aged madness.' Now, there's an example of your double standard!

"I've always had my own money, and my husband left me well provided. If I want to spend some of it on Phil—I bought him a gorgeous briefcase, some shirts and ties, little things—who's to say no? I'm not buying him, keeping him, or exploiting him. I've got the money to use as I desire.

"When I was first widowed, I was surrounded by men. Forget about the ones who were married to my friends. Oh, yes, they were there . . . with their special offers of consolation. I'm talking about the ones who want to latch on to money. I think I'm a better catch than the divorcee. There's no one around, no ex-husband on the scene to provide competition. During the first three years, when I was sorting them all out, I had four proposals; one from a marvelous, dignified man of sixty-nine. A good time for him meant dinner out and home by nine. He believed in that 'early to bed and early to rise' routine and don't exert yourself if it can be avoided. My friends considered him terribly eligible. My question was, 'For what?'

"My children are grown. They're good kids. It took up about twenty years of my life. Now I want to have fun. I want to have a good time. Did I tell you that Phil taught me to dance? I can now eat my cheesecake and not worry about calories.

"And the sex is delicious. I had an early menopause and I was ecstatic. Can you believe that? No more children . . . no more diaphragm. I took a pearl-tipped pin and popped holes through it, creating a crazy design—and laughed like a maniac. I was suddenly sexually free. And if I could have jumped in the air and clicked my heels, I would have. Phil is an aphrodisiac; I can look at him and get turned on. We're very out front about our sex life and deal openly with what pleases the other. Mutual satisfaction is the goal. I sometimes enjoy using the vibrator. Phil has learned exactly how much intensity I can take, and when he uses it on me, I could quite easily go out of my mind!

"I don't want you to get the idea that everything is idyllic or that I'm Little Mary Sunshine. I'm facing the big, half-century mark, and on rainy days there may be some aches and pains and I'll look out this large window and hug myself and worry about getting older and perhaps spending those later years alone.

"I don't have any answers. Perhaps there aren't any. My husband died in ten minutes at the breakfast table. So I'm taking each day as it comes, and wringing out all the joy I can. Right now, Phil is a question mark. Maybe I'm afraid to admit how much he means to me. I don't know what will happen to us. I do know that I'm not going to behave like some other widows I know. I refuse to crawl into a hole and mourn what was. I'm living in the present and loving it!

Norma, 55; Hank, 47. They have been living together for three years.

Norma was a plump woman dressed in a brown, patterned two-piece Arnel outfit. We met in a restaurant, late one afternoon, where she spoke with us for more than an hour. At some moments there was a hysterical quality to her voice, and she began to cry when talking about her son.

"Hank and I have known each other for eight years. We met on jury duty, served on the same case for three weeks, and became friends. He's a well-known free-lance writer. At the time, we were each married, and Hank was living in Greenwich Village.

"I had two kids and a house in the suburbs. I was a gourmet cook, belonged to the League of Women Voters, played bridge, and knit like Mme. Defarge. My friends were living the same kind of life. We even had identical station wagons in the garage—all very typical and very average.

"As my kids grew older, I slowly took college courses, adding credit after credit until I received a B.A. and a master's degree. My husband didn't mind my going to school as long as it didn't interfere with my household duties. If I was there at six to fix him a hot meal, then everything was fine. He had no objection to school, but he didn't want me reading books when he was around.

"School was exciting for me. I hungered for knowledge. Term papers were a challenge and I actually looked forward to exams, to prove to myself how much I had learned. In school I became a person in my own right. I was no longer just a wife and a mother. I felt satisfied with my academic life. With that under control, I began to worry about my emotional one. During this entire time, Hank and I were meeting once a month in the city for lunch. It was all terribly pleasant. We'd share some interesting talk, some good food. That was it.

"So, finally, at forty-seven, I took a good, close look at myself in relation to my marriage. The women's movement couldn't be ignored, and all the reading I had done called out for some kind of personal evaluation. My husband and I had nothing together. Our sex life had evaporated to the point where we had separate bedrooms. We didn't communicate on any subject. The house echoed not with the sounds of talk but with the blaring of the television. We were a non-going, non-doing, nothing kind of couple. I took up space in the house as cook, laundress, cleaning woman. That was the sum total of my existence as the suburban matron, and that seemed to suit my husband just fine. He had his club, tennis, and his golfing buddies, so he was in good shape. 'Enough,' I finally said. After many painful months of examination, I decided I wanted my own life while there was still time. I was granted a divorce the day after my forty-eighth birthday, after twenty-five years of marriage. I remember feeling liberated, but also terribly scared.

"My family has money. I was able to leave my marriage without taking a thing from my husband. I moved into my first apartment, which was three blocks from where Hank was living. Perhaps I felt more comfortable about being on my own, knowing I had a friend close by. That first year, I went into seclusion. I read everything I could get my hands on, went to the theater, to movies, to museums. I was like a person just released from prison. And I did all these things by myself. My children didn't even visit. They were angry and bitter at me for disturbing their lives. I think they felt I should leave them alone with my problems because they were too busy with theirs.

"Hank and I constantly ran into each other in the neighborhood. I felt a very strong attraction to him. It was the first such feeling in twenty years. Sometimes I'd blush; my hands would get cold and clammy. Me, a mature woman, behaving like a teen-ager! At this time he was still married and, uh . . . I was too conventional to suggest an affair, so we remained good friends. From time to time, he'd drop by my apartment to borrow a book, share a cup of coffee. A friend suggested I was running a library, but that was all right with me.

"I finally got my degree, and then Hank just dropped out of sight for two years. I heard from a friend that he had gotten a divorce and was running around with a lot of women. They called them 'Hank's harem.' I was disappointed to lose his friendship and I guess kind of jealous over his social life. Meanwhile, mine had improved. I was dating a few nice men who took me to dinner and afterward to a concert or to a lecture. The men were my age or older. I had very self-conscious-in-the-dark sex with two of them. I felt like I was still a virgin.

"I decided to become active in the community and attended the next meeting of the local planning board. And who should be sitting there in the auditorium drinking coffee, but Hank. Well, we became friends once again and this time sex was involved; gradually the lights came on and stayed on, and sex was like nothing I had ever known. Hank is warm and tender, a marvelous lover. For the first time in my life, I knew the joy of having an orgasm. It wasn't just something I had read about in a book. He slowly started to keep clothes at my apartment until he had a closetful. It wasn't long after that when he moved in . . . bags and books.

"Older women have always played important roles in Hank's life. He was an only child. His father died when he was two years old. His mother and a spinster aunt brought him up. I have never met them, but they call here quite often with instructions for Hank. Every time his mother calls, she is terribly polite and formal. I feel as if I'm the telephone operator at some hotel. Hank still relies on them a great deal. I thought he had been weaned from them, but it's not so. He calls three times a week just to check in.

"My family consists of my two kids. My daughter is married and lives in another state. She calls on my birthday and on Mother's Day. We have never been close; it was a first pregnancy, terribly difficult. She was a sickly child, had a hard adolescence, and never really became an interesting adult; I feel that I am more involved with life than she is.

"My son gave me nothing but grief when he was growing up. He began running away from home when he was ten. He was thrown out of junior high school and three private schools as a discipline problem. My husband couldn't control him. They had a number of really bloody fights. Forget me— he didn't listen to a thing I said. When he was seventeen, he just disappeared. We hired a detective, but he couldn't find him. My heart breaks when I think of his life. I wanted him to see a psychiatrist but he refused. About a year ago, he traced me to this apartment and moved in with his sleeping bag for a few days. He is going to begin college this fall. Maybe he will be a late bloomer, like I was. He was nice to me for the first time, but he was rude and nasty to Hank. He told him to 'shut up' numerous times. And accused me of trying to 'manage' Hank's life as I had tried to do his.

"I'm quite sensitive about my age. In the last few months I've really begun to worry about being in my fifties. All of a sudden I've recognized Hank as being my fountain of youth. Hank's writer and editor friends are all younger. Sometimes I'm jealous of them. I know I can hold my own intellectually, but physically . . . well. He has become my impetus for my own revitalization. I don't want to lose Hank because I'm older than he is. I've cut my hair and started having facials. I even went to a cosmetician to learn how to apply makeup. And I'm determined to lose twenty pounds! I might have eventually done all these things in the course of my own liberation . . . Hank just speeded me along.

"I enjoy being maternal. I worry about Hank, get him through his daily crises, and take pleasure in preparing his favorite foods. A therapist I was seeing a year ago suggested that I was looking for another son to control. I stopped seeing him. If this relationship gives me pleasure and makes me happy, then that's all that counts. At this stage in my life I'm more concerned with my own satisfaction rather than what's motivating it.

"Besides our great sex life, Hank has made an emotional commitment to me. Nobody ever took me seriously or cared about what I was thinking. He does. He accepts me as a person and no one ever did that before."

Alan, 23. He has had more than ten relationships with older women. He is a tall, sandy-haired, well-dressed man appearing at least ten years older. He preferred to talk about older women in general, rather than discuss one particular relationship. He is a stockbroker.

"I am an only child. A rather spoiled one at that. We lived in a large, fifteen-room house in Westchester, where I attended a number of private schools. I was bright and precocious for my age. I've always looked older than I was. At twelve I was already six feet tall. My mother was a bug on manners and I was the very correct, polite little gentleman in the blue blazer with the school emblem.

"The summer I was thirteen, I took a job mowing lawns. My father insisted that it would be good for me, that I'd learn to appreciate the value of a dollar. Boy, was he ever right! One woman was especially nice to me. After I did her lawn, she used to invite me in for cookies and a cold drink. One afternoon, she kissed me on the forehead and I was certain that I was in love. All I remember of her now is that she had long, blond hair and always wore shorts. After that kiss, I had wet dreams for a week. The next time I saw her, we talked for over an hour. She listened while I told her about my school, my friends, and the sports I played. She kissed me on the cheek and I somehow found the nerve to put my hand just above her breast. I thought she would yell at me, but she took my hand and guided it under her shirt. She wasn't wearing a bra. Her breasts were large, her nipples hard. I could feel myself getting an erection. She began touching me, and before I knew what was happening, she had pulled off my pants and we were lying on the couch. I remember feeling very scared, yet excited. I had never seen a naked woman . . . well, only in those girlie magazines that were passed around my boys' school. She kept saying, 'Don't worry. Don't worry. I'll help you! And she did. My God, it was fast! One, two, three, I was in and out. She told me I'd get better with practice. I dressed quickly, feeling very embarrassed, and left. All week, I worried about what would happen when I saw her again. Maybe she wouldn't want me to mention it, or perhaps she'd want me to pretend it didn't happen. So I mowed her lawn, went in for my usual cookies, and then she very calmly said, 'Well, Alan, are you ready for your lesson?' Again we went to the couch. This time she told me a few things to do and guided me with her hands. This weekly relationship lasted for almost four months. I told no one. After all, who would ever believe it? I mean, this woman knew my mother and father! One day when I had completed my garden chores, I went in to have my regular snack and found that everything had changed. To my surprise, she introduced me to her son, who was home from boarding school. He was a year younger than me. We didn't make love that afternoon, and for the next three weeks I made up excuses not to be there. I was devastated by the evidence of her son. I had never thought of a husband or a child, and I just couldn't cope with it. I guess I didn't want to think that she had a whole life that I knew nothing about. I called her on the phone and said I wouldn't be able to work for her any more. She said she was sorry. That was my initial involvement with sex, and with an older woman.

"My parents got divorced when I was fifteen, sold the terrific house I grew up in, and moved into Manhattan. My mother traveled a great deal and I lived with my father until I was seventeen. I moved out because we were always fighting, and got my own place, on the Upper East Side.

"I've wondered why I've always preferred older women. Perhaps because I've always attended boys' schools and there was never an opportunity for me to meet girls my own age. I remember having crushes on some of my women teachers and then had one short affair with my math instructor when I was a sophomore.

"I am drawn to women because of feelings, moods. I believe very strongly in body language. I seem to gravitate to women who are sad-looking, who are usually sitting by themselves looking very much alone. I think I look to be protective. I find women who are floundering and rush in to help.

"When you buy perfume, the package usually looks fantastic but the smell might be phew! Some younger women are very sexually attractive, all you want to do is take them to bed, but that's it . . . that's when the packaging breaks down. You've got to look beyond the physical attraction. Older women have a depth that can't compare to younger women. It's what's inside, rather than what's outside, that counts. I think the majority of men prefer to think with their cocks instead of with their heads.

"My relationships with older women are always marked by a great deal of laughter. I'm an optimist by nature. There is no tomorrow, no yesterday . . . only today. Things you'd fight over with a younger woman, you end up laughing at with an older one, because they really don't mean a thing. To a younger woman, though, they do. Younger women get hurt more easily; they get upset too quickly. They can't appreciate the humor of life.

"With an older woman the conversation is freer, on a more honest level. A younger woman feels she has something to hide. An older woman has every edge. She especially has security of mind. A younger woman doesn't know what she wants, or if she did, she wouldn't know where to go to get it. Older women are secure in the knowledge that they are women. Sometimes you can't even say 'younger women,' for many of them are really young girls. I think, with an older woman, things are on a more trusting level. One time when I was seeing a younger girl, I had to go away on business for three days. She was feeling terribly insecure when I returned and came at me with a barrage of questions. Where did I stay? Who did I see? What did I do? I don't think she wanted to know because she was interested but, rather, because she was insecure about our relationship and thought there might be competition.

"I think that older women sometimes use younger men. It's never happened to me, but I know that this situation exists. Younger men are owned by older women. They're like puppets. It's 'I'll buy your body . . . you'll get your clothes, your apartment, your car. And when I'm no longer happy with you, out you go.' A gigolo is only out for monetary and property gain. There is no emotional or mental involvement. It's all mechanical sex.

"Many of the relationships I've had have caused talk. If you value the people around you, and they're just a little bit different, you're going to get flak. Other people are jealous. I try not to give a damn about what people say, I just give a damn about what I do. When I'm in a relationship, I feel that people can't just accept one of us; they've got to accept us both. I have no friends outside of business. I'm a one-person person. As long as it lasts, that person is my life.

"I would venture to say that an older-woman/younger-man relationship is the strongest one that exists between two people in today's society. There's no opportunity for boredom, no sense of competition. The age difference only gives the relationship immense possibilities for growth.

"I want to get married, and definitely to an older woman."

Rosalind, 48; Ted, 33. They have been married for six years. Ted adopted Rosalind's child (now thirteen) from a previous marriage, two years ago. This is an interracial marriage; Rosalind is black, and Ted is white.

Rosalind wore her graying hair in a becoming, close-cropped Afro. Small and attractive, she was conservatively dressed in a gray flannel skirt and blazer. Ted was tall and bearded, dressed in a pinstriped three-piece suit. Puffing on his pipe, he appeared much older than his actual age.

Ted: Roz was one of my instructors in graduate school. She is now a consultant to a large corporation and I teach part time at the university.

Rosalind: I remember Ted in those early days as a bright, inquisitive, outspoken student. He attempted (somewhat comically, in retrospect) to get me to go to the movies and a variety of other things. I usually succeeded in wriggling out of any dates. I thought he was looking for an older woman to confide in. I was somewhat attracted, but wary, as the father of my child was also a much younger man (fourteen years younger). Age was not mentioned when the initial mutual contact was made. As for physical attraction, I found him not only attractive but often irresistible.

Ted: That's nice to hear after all this time. But believe me, the feeling was reciprocal. It seemed that we went quite quickly from a relationship in which we shared little more than professional activities into one in which we spent most of our time together. We found ourselves to be extremely compatible as a couple, with a very closely shared appreciation of the human condition, although I am an incurable optimist and Roz is an incurable pessimist. Though both insecure in our own ways, we found our neuroses to be complementary, rather than in conflict. By the summer, we had decided to get married. After a series of non-committal relationships, I was ready, I felt, to make a long-term commitment. We were married that fall.

Rosalind: You asked about obstacles. Well, I don't think it was age that was the biggest one, but the fact that Ted was going to marry a black woman. His family was furious. His mother flew here to Boston from California. She pleaded with one of Ted's professors to 'talk some sense' into Ted before it was too late. The professor declined. She also tried to get the family dentist, a friend of long standing, to intervene. He tried, but unsuccessfully.

Ted: I agree. The fact that I am white and she is black has been far more of an obstacle than our difference in age. In the early years of our relationship, we experienced some discrimination in housing, and we continue to feel that finding suitable neighborhoods is a problem.

Rosalind: Let's say that in terms of psychological adjustments, I, as the "older woman," felt very inadequate when I compared myself with younger women—especially white women. All of the middle-aged aches and pains that I suffered seemed hideously magnified. I was especially humiliated because I wear dentures and felt very embarrassed by that. And then there was the adjustment that Ted had to make in regard to becoming an "instant father."

Ted: Sure there was a problem at first. I really knew nothing about child-rearing, and all of a sudden I was placed in the paternal role with a little, six-year-old offspring. The fact that the biological father was also white may have helped matters along. In spite of adapting to the role of father, I do not have the time or energy to devote to raising a large family. My career is more important to me than a brood of children. Roz was in agreement with this from the beginning.

As with any married couple, I suppose, there are sexual jealousies. Roz, though, is more "monogamous" than I, so she is the one who suffers most from jealousy. I have never had an affair, but I have flirted and even behaved in a way to lead Roz to believe that I have wished to cheat on her. When my eye wanders, however, it is not necessarily to younger women.

On the whole, we find ourselves more and more compatible as the years go by—in spite of Rosalind's jealousy. We love to do all kinds of things together. This house, for example, was furnished and decorated as a joint effort; we share household chores equitably; we love to travel together; we enjoy the same kinds of entertainment. We really are our own best friends.

Rosalind: A number of our "other" friends were a little surprised at first by the relationship. Those that have kept in touch throughout the years have always been very supportive. They were neither Ted's "peers" nor mine, falling in the middle between our ages.

The reaction of my parents? Well, they have grown to expect peculiar things of me. They tend to hide reactions to some of my behavior, as if they have no right to an opinion. Their immediate, "surface" reactions were positive, especially after meeting Ted and seeing that he physically appeared to be much older than he in fact is. I guess you could say that by this time they've accepted us. They usually spend two weeks here in the summer.

Ted: You've already heard about my mother. She and my father were so adamantly opposed to our getting married that I cut off all contact with them for about two years. We are now reconciled, exchange visits several times a year, and get along fairly well. The racial issue, I feel, has caused more trouble for my parents than the age difference, and if there is still some tension between us and them, that is the cause of it. My parents have pretty much accepted our child as their grandchild, but that, again, is not so much a function of the relationship between Roz and me as it is a function of the adoption-grandparents syndrome.

In sum, Roz and I are happy and totally committed to one another. Forget race and age and think of us as two people who found each other in a world filled with people who are looking. I think we're damn lucky.

Rosalind: Amen!

Gail, 33; Jeff, 25. The relationship lasted for two years, and presently they are friends.

Gail was an attractive woman, with thick, shoulder-length, black hair. She was slim, of medium height, and modishly dressed in well-fitted jeans, a gray cowl-neck sweater, and a houndstooth blazer. She carried a large Vuitton satchel. Her only makeup was two spots of rouge on her cheeks, contributing to her already healthy and outdoorsy look.

"I first met Jeff through mutual friends. He was nineteen; I was twenty-seven. I seem to remember that maybe six of us spent an afternoon together. I thought he was a nice guy, but that was my only impression. Two years later, we met again at a party and spent the entire evening getting reacquainted. He was temporarily living with his sister in Queens and was looking for his own apartment in Manhattan. I invited him to use my apartment as a base and . . . he just stayed. The days passed. We didn't get in each other's way. We didn't hassle each other. It was really kind of pleasant. He put up some shelves . . . something I'd been meaning to do for months; fixed a leaky faucet, and was Harry Helpful and Charlie Cheerful. So, after about a week, he gave up looking for his own place. No big deal or decision; no firecrackers. We just agreed he should stay. At the time, I was driving a cab. I told my boss about him and he was able to work there too. Living in a studio apartment, we developed a comfortable closeness, which of course involved sex . . . hell, there was only one bed! We began as good friends and grew into lovers.

"I wasn't Jeff's first older woman. When he was fifteen, his high school teacher seduced him. Talk about morality! She picked him up every weekend and all they did was fuck. I guess that's extracurricular activity for you! I should really thank her, though, because Jeff got a great introduction to sex. He's been sexually active now for ten years. He's had numerous affairs with women of all ages, and I think that, just because he was so experienced, he was able to give me tremendous pleasure and satisfaction.

"Since we both worked nights, we had the whole day to play, and boy did we play! Bicycle trips and walks around the city, picnics in the park, the Staten Island ferry for one whole day, movies—sometimes four in a row. You could say we weren't leading a very conventional life. It was constant fun, constant newness, constant movement. We also got into building our own furniture, and Jeff taught me how to refinish some great old pieces we picked up in a thrift shop.

"I wasn't really settled at the time; I didn't know what I wanted, I was just wandering. And Jeff, Jeff was my Peter Pan, promising to take me off to some wonderful never-never land. I was content with him. I loved his wry sense of humor, his fascination with new ideas, his ability to see things from different angles. When I was with him—talking, playing, fooling around—most of the time I never felt an age difference.

"After we had been living together for over a year, I found out that I was pregnant. It was an accident, but I was ecstatic! I was thirty and there had been times when I'd fantasized about having a child and wondered if I wasn't getting too old. I can still remember the day: I was feeling all nice and motherly. That night, I fixed a special dinner, bought wine, lit candles, the whole works! When I told my big important news to Jeff, there was silence. And I kept saying, 'So what do you think, so what do you think?' Finally he said: 'I can't have a baby now. I'm still a baby myself.' With that he got up from the table and walked out. He didn't come home that night and I was frantic. When I called the cab company to say I was sick, they said he had called in too. I decided, around four A.M., to get an abortion. I just had a part-time job and wasn't really ready to assume the responsibilities of mother-hood. Hell, I was still finding myself, and also helping Jeff to do the same. We were in no way, shape, or form ready to be parents, or even marry each other. Okay. So Jeff finally turned up the next afternoon looking very sorrowful and, yes, I had to admit . . . looking terribly young. His arms were filled with flowers, candy, and magazines; as if I were in bed with the flu. I told him about my decision and he seemed relieved, but was quick to add something like: 'Hey, maybe in a few more years when I'm older . . . you know, when I have a reg-ular job.' So, the problem was over, the decision taken out of his hands, and we made love: the end-all, cure-all. The next week, I went for the abortion by myself and we never talked about it again.

"I guess after that we just kind of drifted along for another year. I knew him so well and loved him dearly, but more and more it seemed I was getting progressively edgy. I was an-noyed that his mother would never talk to me when she called. She referred to me as 'that whore on the Lower East Side.' And yet his sister, who was my age, often came to visit us. Sometimes I felt closer to her than I did to Jeff, because she had a definite career and definite goals in mind.

"I was beginning to get bugged that Jeff didn't seem to know what he wanted to do with his life. I mean, he had a college degree and yet was content to keep driving a cab. Meanwhile, I had found a job as a secretary in an advertising agency. I loved my work, found I was good at it, and was looking forward to a promotion. I was becoming 'estab-lishment,' and Jeff seemed to have no ambition at all. In the beginning it had been fun: he was Peter Pan, right? But, more and more, I was feeling that the time for games-only was over. I was starting to feel older, more conservative, more conventional. I wanted him to shape up, to make a decision, to choose some straight job to do and then do it. I wanted him for once to wear a suit instead of a pair of jeans.

"At that time, though, I wasn't into asserting my wishes. I kept them hidden and they just kept eating away at me. I became a nagging bitch for all the wrong reasons. We decided to go into an 'open relationship,' and I started dating men from my office whom Jeff referred to as 'the upper East Side slicks.' The final split, when it came, was really the toll of a gradual breaking away. When he left on a cross-country trip, we both knew that he wouldn't be coming back. We're close now, but there's a difference. For one thing, I've made up for those months of dishonesty by being absolutely candid with him about my present life. He's like a big brother to me now. And his mother accepts me as a legitimate friend, perhaps because I'm no longer a threat, no longer daughter-in-law material. Jeff tells me about the girls he dates, and I think his notion of the perfect woman would *not be* eight years older. I used to feel, when I had an emotional investment in him, threatened when he talked about his social life—not by his young chicks, but if he were to meet someone my own age. After all, I've got years of experience on me, and I feel a woman my age would have more to offer him; therefore, she would be the real competition.

"What did I learn from the good times with Jeff? Well, most of all, to be more open, more accepting of people without making snap judgments. Jeff helped me to see things with fresh eyes, to take delight from everyday things, like just watching a bird build a nest. It may sound hokey, but Jeff helped me grow up and to realize my own potential. Maybe it really was the young-old contrast. There came a time when I knew I didn't want to remain where he was. I knew I was ready to move on.

"Jeff's love made me feel emotionally secure when I was in

my goofing-around period. I hadn't had that many positive experiences with men, and he made me feel I could be a successful part of a couple. Now that I'm happy in my work and feel good about myself, I want to get married and have children. I think Jeff and I will always remain friends."

Owen, 26; Marge, 36. Their relationship is three months old. Marge is married to Owen's cousin.

Owen was a muscular, well-built man with brown hair. Dressed in tight-fitting slacks and a form-fitting tee shirt that showed every flex of his chest and arms, he radiated raw sexuality. He spoke to us in a low, husky voice, seeming to weigh each word.

"I know my situation is strange—after all, she is my cousin's wife. I sometimes feel uneasy about it, but then I try to be objective about the matter. They've been married ten years. My cousin, Steve, is thirty-eight and really in poor physical condition. He just let himself go to flab. He's working all the time: days, nights, weekends. He's not very gregarious and they don't have much of a social life. She's complained that he's cold to her. He's always too tired to make love. She tells me all this about her husband, my cousin, and he's probably the best friend I have. Hell, if only it could have been someone else. I work for him part time and he does me a lot of favors. I sometimes feel like I'm caught in this larger-than-life emotional bind, like I'm an extra in a television soap opera. I think he feels that his marriage is breaking down but prefers to look the other way.

"We'd all been good friends for years, and then one Saturday afternoon everything changed. Steve took a rare day off and we went to a museum, which was very crowded. He was off looking at some paintings in another room. Somehow, the crowd kept pushing Marge and me into each other. There was a lot of eye contact, body contact . . . the works. I seemed to be seeing her for the first time and was very turned on. I kind of hoped she'd make an advance. But no luck! A couple of days later, she called me and said she wanted to talk. When she came over, she looked exhausted. She said she hadn't been sleeping well. And then she bluntly told me that she wasn't having sex with her husband, no sexual release of any kind. She continued by making a direct proposition: 'I like you, Owen. We've always been friends, and Steve wouldn't be hurt. Can you help me out?' There was no more talk. We were going at it hot and heavy fifteen minutes after she arrived. That's how it all began.

"It's just a sexual relationship. I'm convenient, that's all. There's no question of love. We've become close, but it's not a romance. I'm a stud, pure and simple. I even think she likes that fantasy. I know I'm good in bed. My body is as well-tuned as Bruce Jenner's—the Olympic medal winner. Believe me, I can make that woman purr.

"A week ago, we started going out during the day. Before that, she just came over for sex. Now we'll have sex and then walk around, have lunch, maybe go to a movie. She's too sophisticated for my friends, and I don't really fit into her circle. But she's got the perfect cover. If anyone sees us, she can always introduce me as her cousin, and no one would be the wiser!

"I have a number of women friends my own age, but at this time there's nothing sexual going on. I feel too caught up in this thing with Marge to start something new. I think I am definitely attracted to older women who are already in some way fulfilled. Older women seem much more desirable. They appear more conscious of their sexuality. Also, older women can provide a wiser kind of guidance for the whole relationship. I think I also enjoy the idea of competition, of a challenge. I'm providing good sex. It's not casual. I would hope that she'd wake up in the middle of the night and think: 'Gee, I wish he were here.' With someone older, you're called upon to perform more—sexually and emotionally.

"My friends wouldn't understand this affair. An older woman, yes; married, no. I've probably exercised more discretion, in this affair, than with anyone else. Other times, it was too much a source of pride not to talk about it. Now silence is a necessity, and that probably adds to the excitement of this relationship.

"I think, if my mother knew, she'd have a heart attack. Well, not exactly, but I do think she'd feel competitive. I'm speaking now just of age. She'd probably try to come between us. I imagine she sees me with a nice, young girl. You know, society's ideal of the older man and the younger woman. And when I visualize myself married, it's to someone my own age. I wonder if that's a cop-out after everything I've said. Anyway, I left home when I was sixteen, so maybe I am looking to Marge for some kind of mothering. I'm not really sure.

"Marge looks old. She seems to have aged considerably in the last few months. I've noticed wrinkles on her forehead and circles under her eyes, but her body's still in good shape. I've never really felt any difference in a woman's body if she's in condition, whether she's twenty-five or forty.

"Biologically, I think we've got a good thing going, for the time being. There's no question of her marriage breaking up at this time. They both seem content to let it drift. And if it did end, well, I wouldn't know what I'd do with her. So for now we're content with what we have: a good sexual relationship. That's okay for me."

Marion, 53; Don, 37. They have been living together for seven years.

Marion wore her steel-gray hair in a becoming French twist. Tall and stately at five ten, she was elegantly dressed in a navy-blue-and-white wrap dress. She wore tiny pearl earrings with a matching strand around her neck. We talked to her in her law office—a spacious modern room decorated in warm earth colors and filled with plants and trees.

"I got married when I was thirty-one—rather late for the times. I suppose I waited so long because of my career. I desperately wanted to become a lawyer and was the first woman this firm hired. My ex-husband was also a lawyer—a long-time bachelor of forty when we met. We were together for twelve years and we're still friends—in a professional sense. I think we gravitated toward each other because we were lonely and we kept getting paired off at all the dinner parties in town. Everyone thought we were both so eligible and right for one another. I guess after a while we began to believe so too.

"Tom and I were workaholics in those days. Home was a place to eat dinner, discuss our cases, and then retire to our individual studies to prepare for the following day in court. We were first and foremost good friends . . . professional colleagues.

"At the time, I still had a residue of Catholic-school craziness. All those nuns, all those years of being a pure little schoolgirl, only to be followed by many years of being the good, faithful wife. I'd learned my early lessons well, and suppression of any kind of sexual feeling was the name of the game. Tom was sexually uninformed when we got married and didn't bother to learn anything new during the twelve years we were together. It was fumble, grope, insert, sleep—an early pattern that never changed. Thank God, I did! Can you imagine, I thought that was what sex was all about.

"As the years passed, Tom began spending more and more of his time out on the Coast, handling clients in the film industry. He'd be there six weeks, here for ten days, and back out there for two months. For the last year of our marriage, we only touched base perhaps five weeks in total. We got a friendly divorce when he moved his practice, because the commute was getting ridiculous. I think now that our marriage was one of planned convenience. It wasn't a love affair. When it was good, it was just comfortable camaraderie.

"Eight years ago, a friend asked me to handle the closing on a town house in Georgetown for a friend of his. It was a favor. The house was being bought by a sociology professor at American University.

"When I first met Don, I was forty-five and he was twenty-nine. I thought he looked like he was forty and he thought I looked thirty-five. I guess it was wishful thinking on both our parts. Don is six two and very good-looking. I was sexually turned on just seeing him across the room. You have to realize that these were relatively new feelings for me, and I wasn't sure what to do with them. So for three weeks I just enjoyed fantasizing.

"The night we closed the deal on his house, I took him out to dinner to celebrate. I drank too much wine and was feeling pleasantly high and relaxed. We went back to my place and necked on the couch like teenagers. I was getting more and more aroused, when he picked me up in his arms and carried me into the bedroom. He undressed me so slowly. It was pure torture having his hands all over my body when all I wanted was him inside of me. At first I felt all elbows and knees—the real middle-aged maiden. You know the saying 'Blow in her ear and she'll follow you anywhere'? Well, that's what stands out when I think of the first time we made love. It almost drove me crazy. I tingled right down to my toes. And then it was over so quickly I couldn't believe it. The second time we made love, I had an orgasm. And then I started crying . . . from joy.

"The next morning, I was late to my office—the first time in eight years. Of greater significance was this incredible feeling that I was in love, gloriously, rapturously, head-over-heels, for the first time in my life—at forty-five—in love! I can feel myself blushing even now, just thinking about that day. I don't think I got a thing done. I just sat in this office smiling and mooning like a teen-ager. I remember leaving early to buy a new dress. That seemed terribly important at the time.

"That first year of being together—we were inseparable—

were equal parts ecstacy and hell. I couldn't imagine it lasting. I'd think, if it lasted six months, then I'm six months ahead, and if it lasted a year, then I'm a year ahead. I just couldn't wipe out those sixteen years so fast. And yet, Don's very untypical. He was just born grown up. There are people like that, you know. You wonder what happened to their childhood.

"I was very uneasy meeting his friends. But some of them were very impressed with the fact that I was a lawyer. Those that didn't care about me, or about us together, well, as time went on they just peeled away. Most of my friends accepted him; I think they were forced to if they wanted to remain my friend. And if they truly cared about me, what made me happy, and they were aware that he was the source of my happiness, then the caring had to be extended to him.

"After a monogamous year, we bought a house together. We had talked about it for a long time, and it was a well-thought-out commitment made on both our parts. We've been living together now for seven years, and I'd be lying if I didn't say I've never thought of him leaving me for someone younger. He doesn't want children, so I know that wouldn't be the attraction. It would have to be something more. Perhaps because he's younger, I'm more on my toes. He's terribly handsome and I'm terribly vain. If you think I'd let myself—my looks, my figure, my hair—go, so that he would be attracted to a younger woman, that he'd want to wander, or have a reason to— well then, you're out of your mind. By taking good care of me, I'm taking good care of us.

"And now that I'm a partner in this firm, I don't have the need to be so competitive, so driven in my work, the way I was with Tom. I have the time to be with Don, to listen when he talks about his students, to proofread the papers he writes for his professional journals, and to take off to attend his sociology conventions, which are like mini-vacations for us. I can give more of myself, because I'm not so hell-bent on my own achievement. I've done it. I've made my mark. I don't have to prove anything to anybody. Don doesn't treat me like a sex object. He doesn't treat me like a mother. He treats me . . . like I was . . . a person of value. And through the years, I have learned how to relax in the comfort of the two of us together."

Grace, 41; Bill, 21. They have been living together for three years.

Grace was a small, fine-boned, light-skinned black woman. She was dressed modishly in a three-piece pants suit. Large horn-rimmed glasses gave her a somewhat bookish appearance. She spoke with beaming pride of her relationship with Bill, showing us a number of pictures of the two of them.

"Bill was a student in the high school where I was a guidance counselor. He came to me at the end of his junior year to plan his next year's program. I often noticed him in the halls— you had to, because he was a standout. He was six feet two inches tall. We became speaking friends during his senior year. I think we both felt something was there, but we didn't dare approach it until he was about to graduate. I often took groups of students to plays and lectures and always invited him, but he never came. I tried to include him in my outside social life, but he backed off. He never showed up. I gave a party for some of the graduating seniors, and he finally attended. We left for a while and went outside, where we walked and talked and walked and talked. I felt like I'd known him for ages. When we came back, my daughter was very upset, because the party was over and I hadn't said good night to my guests. My daughter is very proper.

"I think I was first attracted to Bill's body. He was a karate champion, in fantastic shape. He used to wear tight-fitting tee shirts that showed off every one of his muscles. The guy just didn't have an ounce of fat on him. He exuded sensuality. He never overtly approached me. I was the aggressor all the way.

"A week after the party, I invited him to my house. He arrived sometime in the afternoon. We talked for a damn long time and nothing physical happened. It was getting late and I was afraid my daughter would be home soon. So at some point I just said: 'Why don't we go into the bedroom?' and then, 'Why don't we take our clothes off?' That was it. I seduced, or, rather, encouraged our first sexual involvement.

"The next week, I went to a party at his mother's house. He said he wanted me to meet what there was of his family. I didn't quite know how to act. I was his guidance counselor, his lover. But who was I really, and what part would I play in his life? Anyway, all my worrying was for nothing, Everything turned out okay. I mean, they just accepted me as a person.

"Later in our relationship, when my daughter discovered we were lovers, things got quite messy. She wouldn't speak to him. They each talked to me but not to one another. Although she didn't say it outright, I'm sure she felt threatened and perhaps shocked that I was in love with someone her own age. She never really tried to stop me, but I imagined her thinking: 'Mothers don't do that sort of thing.' Even though she knew I was a liberal parent, I think she thought I was carrying it too far. Yet she didn't make any direct remarks.

"Bill went off to college and spent vacations and spare weekends with me. We sort of slid into living together. Gradually, more and more of his belongings were kept at my house. I missed him terribly when he was away. I guess that was when I realized how much I loved him.

"Bill is a very withdrawn person, because he had so many difficult years when he was growing up. His parents split when he was twelve. He was raised by his father, who's a horribly unpleasant man. After a long separation from his mother, he finally started talking to her when he was seventeen. They are friends now.

"I realize that I look young, and that works in my favor.

Yet I felt very insecure when Bill was away at college. I kept thinking of him with all those gorgeous, twenty-year-old women. When I went up to see him, they knew all the latest dances and I just sat there feeling like some out-of-place old lady. Then, when he was with my friends, he said he felt out of place. But you know what happened? It was all a matter of time. We were together; he was my man, I was his woman, and gradually, everyone accepted us. When he totally relaxed, so did I.

"I use his last name now, so everyone thinks we're married. First he introduced me as his girlfriend, then he began introducing me as his wife. I think that when I'm very insecure I consider marriage. Then I feel I need that piece of paper. I've been married and divorced twice before, so the act also has some very negative feelings for me. I think we're close enough not to rely on a piece of paper to make it all nice and proper and good. Hell, it is!

"Sex has changed to plain old married, everyday sex. It just sort of lost its sparkle and tingle and bells. In the beginning, I thought I was the one who was supposed to teach him, but the third time we went to bed, he was incredibly good and I wondered just where he had learned. I think that older women and younger men are very sexually compatible.

"I've had two one-night affairs. Bill has been faithful. If he knew about my affairs he'd be very jealous, hurt, wounded to the core. I think part of his attitude is due to youth. He doesn't drink; he doesn't smoke cigarettes or pot. I do all three things, and he wishes I didn't. I think his picture of an ideal woman is someone without any of those vices.

"I couldn't have started this relationship with any eighteen-year-old. Bill is a very special person. He finished college in two and a half years, got his master's in six months, and is presently working on his doctorate. He's a genius.

"At first I thought I was the parent in this relationship. I am still the parent at times, because I'm the one with more experience. I'm learning from him, though, all the time.

Maybe it's a combination of therapy, Bill, and simply that as I get older, I'm willing to give and take on a more equal basis.

"Since he's a student, he doesn't make any money. I'm often resentful of that. I don't like 'keeping' him. I'll say: 'Look, you have twenty more years, I don't have twenty more years.' He knows that it's unfair of him. I'm supposed to be responsible for all these bills. We've decided that he's going to take a part-time job. I think I'll feel better then.

"The thought of there being some other woman often crosses my mind. If she were younger, that would threaten me, because there is absolutely nothing I can do with that. If she were older, it wouldn't be the age . . . and that would really bother me. I think I could compete favorably with a younger woman. I'd have to consider someone my own age as a really serious threat.

"I think you have to direct and guide a younger man. That's a plus advantage for an older woman. She's got the experience and she can be a successful teacher. Then, there are other times, when an older woman must be smart enough to lay off and give the guy a chance to grow. And if she's lucky, she will grow too."

Karen, 34; Bill, 25. They have been having an affair for six and a half months.

We met Karen at her apartment, where she had just returned from jogging in Central Park. She was dressed in a navy blue warm-up suit under which she wore a bright red tee shirt. Her face was flushed, her long brown hair tied in a pony tail with a red yarn ribbon. She wore no makeup and looked to be in her mid-twenties.

"I seem to follow a pattern where I always feel a little down after the first of the year, so this time I decided to do something constructive about it. I flew to Puerto Rico for a long weekend, and that's where I met Bill. I was playing roulette in the hotel's casino, and he came and sat down next to me. He didn't look particularly young or old. He was just a nice-looking man who suddenly started winning. His excitement was contagious. In a little while the whole table was friendly and joking and laughing with the croupier. Luckily we didn't have any serious players with us. We all just seemed to be out for a few hours of fun—a good time. I left the table first and went into the bar for a nightcap. It was around midnight. About fifteen minutes later, Bill came in. I saw him look around. He waved and walked over to me and we started talking. We closed the bar at three in the morning and agreed to meet the next day for lunch.

"We didn't discuss any age-related concerns that I can remember. We were surprised and pleased to learn that we both worked in the publishing field. We had a number of friends in common and shared similar work-related problems. Bill mentioned that he lived in Brooklyn and wanted to move to Manhattan, but I never suspected that he still lived with his parents! I felt a definite attraction, but there was no pressure from Bill to sleep with him that first evening, and I liked that.

"We spent the next two days and evenings together. We swam, played tennis, and went into San Juan to shop. We took a bus tour and a boat tour and went disco dancing after playing each night in the casino.

"Bill was very attentive. He's a *touchy-feelie* kind of person. He held my hand, stroked my back, ruffled my hair. I liked his show of affection, the fact that he was so comfortable being physical. It was like a prelude to foreplay, and I was eager for us to make love. Since I'm a good size twelve, I prefer being with a big man. Bill is over six feet tall. He's in excellent shape; he runs, works out in a gym, and is terribly aware of his body. He's got wavy brown hair and blue eyes. He wears horn-rimmed glasses, which I think contributes to the feeling that he's of an indeterminable age.

"Finally, we made love, the night before I left, and it was

memorable. Bill was a gentle, tender lover, making sure that I was pleasured and satisfied before coming himself. We made love three times, and each time, it was different, better. I can't really explain it to you except to say that here was a man who was a giver, not a taker. And believe me, I've been around. I've had enough lovers to make comparisons. Bill didn't just get his rocks off and turn over and go to sleep. When we did finally settle down, it was with my head cradled on his chest, his arm around my shoulder. I felt secure, taken care of, protected. It was a wonderful feeling and different from all those macho men who were nothing more than a total of practiced technique. Or the few men I'd dated in their late forties, where I had been the giver.

"Bill had planned to stay for a week but flew back with me instead. It was on the plane when I learned he was twenty-five. We were talking about college and he told me he had graduated four years before. Shocked? Surprised? Stunned? I was all three. He didn't seem disturbed that I was nine years his senior. It was in my head that the arithmetic games were being played: like, when I was starting college he was in fourth grade, or when I was going to graduate school he was probably just starting to date, and had pimples besides! I wondered what my friends would say, what my mother would think, and if this so changed things, would I want to see him again.

"You know by now that I did. It was rough. I'm not going to claim it wasn't. The missing nine years were hard to erase, so I just began filling him in on *my* times. He soaked up my experiences like a sponge. For instance, I taught him about Vietnam, Vladimir Horowitz, and Brie cheese. And he filled me in on growing up in a permissive climate where he had been initiated into sex when he was fifteen. He also introduced me to Doonesbury and Bruce Springsteen. There are still moments of frustration for me: I'll sing a song he's never heard of, or expect him to choose a wine for dinner and he will select whatever is cheapest. Suave and sophisticated he's not. But, emotionally, there's really no gap. If we didn't care about each other, or respect each other as much as we do, it wouldn't be worth the effort or the static we've had to put up with.

"Bill has moved into the city, a block away from here. I helped him decorate his apartment. His folks wanted to know why the big rush. He's told them he's seeing someone, but they don't know about the age difference. My friends were first disapproving, then they thought it was cute; happy that I had someone to play with, and now that we've been together for some time, and really so obviously enjoy each other's company, I think a few of them are truly envious. My men friends have accepted him totally. Being in the same field of work is a tremendous equalizer.

"If I were a man and he were a woman, everyone would probably congratulate us both. With the tables turned, it's a different ball game. My mother liked him the moment she met him. When she found out how old he was, she took me aside and said, 'What a pity he's not older,' thereby canceling him out of the running. Again, it doesn't matter to others if we're compatible, or if we look good together, which we do. It's just the fact of those lousy nine years. Reverse the sexes and no one would say a thing.

"I've got to admit that it's a turn-on, being adored. It's fantastic for the ego to have someone admire you, to be placed on a pedestal; or, as Bill sometimes says to me, 'God, you're neat!'

"Because of age and experience, I tend to make a lot of the decisions. We've talked about this and now share some of that power that for a while I was holding on to. There are times when I'd like him to be more forceful, more assertive, and maybe it's something he will grow into. Or perhaps that's just my problem—my role conditioning, where the man is in a take-charge position. It could be that once you enter any kind of unconventional relationship, all your actions and ways of looking at things undergo scrutiny. But this, I think, the self-examination, is really what growth is all about. I can't tell you if we'll be together six months from now; perhaps you should do a follow-up book and get back to me. At this moment, Bill and I are working on a relationship that has meaning and growth potential. We are totally aware of the problems, the pluses, and of each other. If we can continue to be honest, share all the feelings, both negative and positive, then I don't see any reason for us to break up. You don't give back a premature baby, do you? You just nourish it and love it and watch it thrive and grow."

Beverly, 60; Jim, 43. Beverly has been having an affair with Jim for the past four months.

Beverly, who was average-looking, had reddish-brown hair and a nice figure. She wore a simple, tailored navy blue dress. Her vivaciousness and zest for life were reflected when she talked. She expressed her thoughts with a variety of facial gestures and hand movements.

"I'd like to tell you about loneliness—the kind that grips you around the heart at four in the morning when you sleep alone. If you're like me, you'll get up from bed, eat some soup, and catch up on your reading. I have a two-bedroom apartment. I'm lucky I have enough space to walk around in. I'll walk, repot plants, go through old magazines, do some needlepoint. The hours pass; sometimes quickly, sometimes slowly.

"I was widowed two years ago. It was my second marriage. There was enough money through insurance and investments so that I don't have to work. But maybe that's a burden, rather than a blessing.

"For the first year without Neal, I stuck pretty close to home. I played bridge every Tuesday night, went to Wednesday matinees, had my hair done on Thursdays, and met the girls for a fancy lunch on Fridays. Sometimes I'd go to a concert or a lecture on Sundays. Not a terribly exciting existence.

"One sleepless night, I was reading the paper and found a news story about older women who went back to college and got credit for their 'life experience.' And I thought, hey, that's for me. I had graduated from high school, was a secretary, then married and lived with my husband, an electrical engineer, in Morocco, Africa, Sweden, and on a kibbutz in Israel. I had three children in three different countries.

"Two months after we returned to the States, my husband left me for a younger woman. I went back to work as a secretary to a doctor. He was a widower and I eventually married him. We had sixteen happy years and a final year that brought us closer than I thought possible, when I watched him die from cancer.

"Neal used to say I was the best-read insomniac around. He'd be unhappy about the way I was spending my time. We were always so active. I remember a vacation in Miami—the resting place of the elderly. We vowed we'd never be like the men and women we saw: filling their days with endless card games, sun worshiping, and Monday-night bingo.

"Now, where was I? Oh, yes, the story in the paper. Well, I applied. I thought if they accepted me, I'd go. Why not get a college degree? So what if I were a fifty-nine-year-old freshman—is that freshperson? I had to go for an interview and write an essay about my goals in life and then I forgot about it. Three months later, I got this long, official-looking envelope in the mail. I remember staring at it on the dining-room table. My life was such a blah at the time. I felt like a traitor to Neal's memory—almost ready to take that plane to Miami. I just wasn't sure I could deal with bad news. And then I started to laugh, remembering how my children felt—when they were waiting to hear from their schools. So, with trepidation, I finally opened the envelope—and you guessed it, I was in with the advanced status of a sophomore!

"I've just completed my first year and it's been very

difficult. I was sure I'd be the only older person there, but I'm not alone. I have a lot of classmates my age and older—who have decided to go for that sheepskin. It's exciting and hard at the same time. Exciting because I'm being exposed to new points of view, ideas that I've never thought of before. Hard because all of a sudden I've been thrown into a new world. I've got mountains of books to read, papers to write, exams to study for. The library had become my second home. But the biggest bonus of returning to school was—"

(The doorbell rang as if on cue. A pleasant-looking man entered. Of medium height, he was dressed in gray slacks and a red turtleneck sweater. His brown hair was lightly sprinkled with gray. Bev proudly introduced us to Jim, her English professor. He was forty-three.)

Jim: Bev took my class the first semester, and then, in the second term, when she was no longer my student, we began to date. I think I was impressed with her wide range of knowledge, her probing questions, and her great sense of humor. There were numerous times when she made the whole class laugh at itself—when we were taking ourselves too seriously.

We used to meet for coffee and just talk. Bev is a great listener. She was interested in my other classes, the books I was reading, the novel I am in the process of writing.

I originally thought she was about fifty. I wasn't hung up on age, although I was taken aback when we celebrated her birthday last month and she told me she was sixty. But then I figured that Bev the person was more important than Bev the number sixty. It hadn't gotten in our way before, and just because it was out in the open, there was no need for us to change anything.

I like Bev. I enjoy being with her. She's absolutely honest. And when I marvel at her forthrightness, her ability to be sometimes . . . too outspoken for her own good, well, then, she'll use her age as a defense, like "I'm too old to fool around with word games. If I feel like saying something, why not say it?"

I got the flu this year and was out for ten days. Bev was at my place every morning and returned after her classes. She slept on the couch because she didn't want to disturb me. She's a gentle, caring woman. Maybe that's the key. She's a grown-up, adult woman; she's not into man-woman coquettish games.

I don't think she was looking for a romance, or a quickie affair. She's not the type. What happened to us could happen to any man and woman who meet, develop a friendship, and see it flower into something infinitely more precious.

Beverly: I told you there was a bonus in going to college at my age! Jim has been wonderful for me. He's opened up a whole new world for me.

And as far as our sex life, well, I'm not ready to pack it in and enter a retirement home. I enjoy sex; the actual act and the foreplay and cuddling warmth that comes after. I'm a compulsive toucher. I talk with my hands. I'll reach over to touch him when I make a point. And I'm not above a game of kneesies played under the tablecloth at a restaurant. It's just another way of saying to Jim that I like him and that I'm happy.

I think male company is important to a woman at any age. I'm more aware now of how I look, of how I dress. I'm pampering myself with creams and oils—something I never did before. I want to be attractive to him. I want him to feel proud of me when we go out together. Jim is friend and lover and I'm grateful we've found each other.

My oldest child is forty. The rest are in their thirties. They are mature enough to accept our relationship and be happy for me, because, because of it, I'm happy.

Sixty is young. It's all in how you see it.

2

FROM A MALE POINT OF VIEW

One of the most interesting discoveries resulting from the interviews with men who sought out and courted older women was that they each had had a very pleasurable sexual experience with a much older woman when they were adolescents. (In most cases, this was the way in which they lost their virginity.) The woman was either a neighbor or a teacher or, in several cases, the mother of the girl they dated. The encounter was always recalled years later with the greatest of satisfaction, as in the following case, in which it is remembered as the most pleasurable sexual experience the man has ever had.

> I was fifteen and a virgin. I was dating her daughter, who was about my age. One evening, I called for my girl only to be told by her mother that she wasn't ready. There was a slow record on the phonograph and the mother asked me if I knew how to dance. When I said no, she offered to teach me. She was dressed in a very sexy pants outfit, and when we danced she held me very tight. Her nipples felt erect under her blouse, and to my great embarrassment, I started to get an erection. I didn't know what to do. I began to sweat and I knew my face was flushed. She noticed what was happening and told me that it was all normal and healthy. She said I should be proud of myself. Two nights later, she called and asked me to come over. Her husband was on the road a great deal, and her daughter (who I'd already forgotten about) was sleeping at a friend's house. As soon as I arrived, she took me by the hand and we began to make love. She was tender and

understanding and showed me what I needed to know. She guided me and taught me what a woman wants. She was a marvelous teacher, and I loved her.

We would meet in the church parking lot several times a week and drive to someplace deserted. The relationship lasted almost a year. I've never forgotten the slightest thing about her. I'm now thirty-one, and though I've been in love since (also with an older woman), I can't recall ever feeling such a degree of sexual intensity.

Is this recollection colored by nostalgia? A longing to recapture lost memories and glories? A romanticizing of one's past? Perhaps. But the man who is speaking is now past thirty. He has a master's degree in business and has known and dated many, many women, and still he cannot recall ever feeling such passion.

Paul Theroux has written that the older woman gives a man the chance to complete in adulthood what was impossible to complete as a child. She awakens his earliest sexual memory. . . . "That friend of one's mother who visited and left an odor of perfume and cigarette smoke and an aphrodisiac smudge of lipstick on her gin glass. That first schoolteacher you wanted to go to bed with, the first woman who gave you informed encouragement and knew what was happening to you, even if you didn't—she was always older and always the ideal. . . ."[1]

What is happening now is that the ideal is becoming the reality. Everyone is coming out. People are not afraid to try on their fantasies, and many of them are finding, to their surprise and joy, that the relationship works, better than they ever dreamed.

In Victorian times, we had the image of the young man of the house chasing the older maid up the staircase for a quickie romp in the hay. Anthropologist Dr. Donald Marshall has written about a whole culture in Polynesia who practice as a basic rite of passage, older-woman/younger-man pairings. "On the Polynesian island of Mangaia," Dr. Marshall writes, there's no such thing as either a man or a woman having a sexual problem. Sex education for the Mangaian youth begins early in adolescence. He is instructed through the use of stories and then is given more "practical" exercises.

The sex, which is always arranged by an expert, must be with an experienced woman. The woman, who is of course older, teaches him techniques involved in carrying out various acts and positions. The male aims for the woman to have two to three orgasms to his one. On the last day of the young man's instruction a feast is given for the boy and his mentor. Only now is he deemed ready to be treated as a man by his people. Only now that he's proved his skills, and his mentor has pronounced him graduated, is he allowed to have sex with a woman his own age or younger.[2]

There is no such rite of passage in American or Western European society. The French, who have always been thought most liberal in their attitude toward older-woman/ younger-man liaisons, had, as recently as 1970, a *scandale célèbre* that ended tragically.

A thirty-one-year-old professor of philosophy in Marseilles, Gabrièle Russier, fell in love with a student, Christian Rossi, age sixteen. They began to live together off campus. When the parents of the student found out, they became enraged, and when their son refused to leave Ms. Russier, they complained to the university, which promptly fired her. The story was picked up by the newspapers, and the scandal that ensued led to her suicide. (In 1972, a movie was made of the story, *Mourir d'Amour*, starring Annie Girardot.)

Not as tragic in its outcome but also extreme in reaction is the following, in which the teacher was also dismissed.

Southold, L.I. Jan. 14 (AP). A high school art teacher who was suspended for marrying one of her students has accepted a $35,000 settlement for dropping her lawsuit against the local school board and agreed to end her campaign to be reinstated.

The teacher, Linda DiPrima, 29 years old, married one of

her students, John Yedloutschnig, 18, of Southold, in August 1976, two months after he graduated.

On September 6, 1976, she was suspended by the Southold school board. The board said it found fault with her association with the student prior to his graduation. . . .

Mrs. Yedloutschnig sued the school board for $1 million and demanded that she be reinstated.[3]

Why the outrage? Why should such a happening even be a news item? Certainly an eleven-year age difference cannot be held up as being something extraordinary. Could we imagine this occurring if the older person had been a man and the younger a woman? Not likely. It seems these reverse May-December liaisons threaten many persons' concepts of the way things should be—the unspoken rules that govern socially approved modes of behavior. In practically all societies, the man is expected to be the achiever, the income bringer, the person who's going to do the taking care of. The veritable rock to your moss, if you will. But when he's with a woman who's older, there's a very good chance that she'll also be richer and more successful. So how, then, is he to fulfill his proper role? And how is society to view both him and the relationship? Often even the participants are unsure.

Richard—age 20, college student:

"I've had this relationship for three years. I first met her when she taught high school in the town I grew up in. Previous to meeting her, I had relationships with six other older females—none sexual. I've always been more at ease with women older than myself; usually from two to nine years older. . . . My present relationship is indeed normal and is serious in the sense that I've proposed numerous times and she's accepted but then changed her mind.

"We are not a weird couple. We communicate better than most couples I know. I am not her son, she is not my mother. We have normal sex.

"I'm an undergraduate math major at a New England university. She's a doctoral candidate just short a few credits at another school. We delayed any physical relationship until two weeks before my graduation, and a real (not just platonic or passionate) relationship seemed to develop about a year after I met her. We lived together while we were students. At first, though I adored her, we weren't on the same emotional plane. She was suffering the emotional disappointments of the failure of her first marriage. We're living apart now, but she'll be coming to join me for the summer and probably for a whole year while I finish school. I'd like to marry her, but she's afraid I'll wake up and ask myself what I'm doing with a woman nine years my senior. I tell her that our relationship isn't so much different from my sister's! She married a man nearly as old as my father last year. . . ."

Dr. Wayne Myers, professor of psychology at Cornell Medical Center, states that the paradigm of a young man using the older woman for experiential purposes and then feeling confident enough to move back to a peer relationship may be related to the increase in sexual freedom and aggressivity in women who are now expressing their appetites at a younger age. The men are frightened by their peer-group women and therefore are seeking out the older, reassuring maternal surrogate to teach or indoctrinate them into the mysteries of the conjugal couch.

Gary—age 22, engineer:

Describing his relationship with a divorced woman of thirty-five who had a daughter of eighteen:

"She instigated it by catching my glance and smiling. At first, I think I was more impressed by her aggressiveness than her age, but the idea of being with an older woman shortly became my major concern. And this was only because I figured it would be something different or novel; I probably would have felt the same if she were my age but of a different skin color.* It was going to be something new and, in a way, like a time machine. I was going to be able to see what most of my lovers might be like ten years from now.

"I think she was more fascinated by my youth than I was about her age. My reaction toward her body was relatively the same as it would have been to anyone else, excepting a natural curiosity as to how a woman looks at her age. I didn't make any vocal comments about her looks, because I thought she might attach some special meaning to what I said. I certainly thought she was beautiful; a mature, graceful kind of beauty, but if I said so, I was afraid she'd think me a silly, lovesick kid or something.

"She was obviously more experienced sexually than I was. I wanted to demonstrate my uninhibited inventiveness in bed more than 'youthful endurance.' We both had something special to give. I guess I did have that 'youthful endurance,' and she was quite able to satisfy my curiosity about things I had little experience in but always wanted to explore more thoroughly. Actually, we both demonstrated on one another that we were sexually creative. I think we were both saying, 'Look how much fun I can be!'

"Very few of my friends knew about this relationship—not because I was embarrassed by it but because I rarely discuss my love affairs with my friends. I fixed up my best friend with hers (also older) and talked with him a little about it. He seemed to feel that older women are better than our own age group, because they don't play the 'mind games' that our contemporary females do. I tend to agree with him on that.

"This was my first experience with an older woman. We lasted four months. I may try it again shortly with a woman I've recently met who's now going through divorce proceedings."

Francine du Plessix Gray has written that young Americans are said to be turning to older women just as access to their

* About 10% of our older woman–younger man relationships crossed racial lines and over 60% crossed religious or ethnic barriers.

contemporaries has reached an unprecedented level of permissiveness. Could it be that the sheltering warmth of a (still partially taboo) Mrs. Robinson can be more mysterious and reassuring to some recent Graduates than the readily available classmates in striped pajamas whom they encounter in shared dorms?[4] The idea of an older woman contributing to the younger man's sexual education and preparing him for later domestic life was one we frequently encountered among men in their twenties.

Howard—age 23, photographer:

"I like older women because young girls want to change me. I'm just looking for someone to accept me the way I am. Older women are willing to do that. Someday, I may make a great husband for a young girl but not now. I'm not ready."

Martin—age 23, filmmaker and student:

"I thought it would be terrific if I could move in with Susan. She's together and she's been a homemaker and she's a lady of experience and what more do I want to live with? She knows how to keep house, to cook, to take care of someone. I can learn from her and when I finally do settle down and marry, I'll be great at it.

"Susan is training me and I like it. Even if we broke up tomorrow, I'd still prefer older women at this stage of my life. They have more to give sexually than a girl my own age, and with an older woman you both know what the moves are, there's no game playing. You can make it flow."

Andrew—age 25, broker:

"I've always thought of myself as older than my years. When I was a kid I used to visit girlfriends' houses and spend half my time talking to their mothers, because I could relate to them better. I have very little to talk about with people my own age. I don't relate to them. From the time I graduated high school, I sought older friends, men and women."

William—age 24, anthropologist:
"Women of a certain age don't worry about taking their image to bed with them. They're interested in a good trip and don't worry about the way they should look according to the latest magazine or news article they've been reading. Kids of twenty or thirty aren't that good in bed. But women of thirty-five to forty-five are generally more apt to please."

Richard—age 24, taxicab driver studying for master's:
"Barbara is an experience for me. That's how I think about our relationship. I have this notion in my head that someday I'm going to meet this perfect woman. She's going to come along and supply everything I want and need. And while I care a great deal about Barb, my perfect lady just doesn't happen to be eleven years older than I am. But, for now, she's great."

Clinical therapist Dr. Penelope Russianoff believes that: "Men often view easy, comfortable, free sex as something that is much more likely with an older woman. Also, a man may not want children and relates better to a woman who has already had her family. A man marrying an older woman would probably be choosing her because of similar interests which they could pursue together. If he wants to train to become a professional, the older woman is not the little woman who is upset if he doesn't come home every evening to baby-sit her, and entertain her, and take care of her. The older woman probably is attractive to him because she has already developed her own involvements and interests."[5]

Sex counselor and therapist Arline Rubin feels: the younger

man doesn't have to be on such a performance trip, since the older woman may be more patient than the younger woman—who might be expecting that the male take the initiative. This kind of relationship, between a younger man and an older woman, has a certain unknown quality about it, a kind of adventurousness where the people involved don't know quite what to expect.[6]

There appear to be as many reasons for older-woman/younger-man pairings as there are people involved. Perhaps age should not be determined as much by a number as by the individual's life purpose.

Some of the men we interviewed felt that they were turned on to older women because those who were the same age were always competing. On a date, there was the game of one-upmanship: her status in her office compared to his. Her salary versus his earning capacity. Did he feel that her career advancement was as important as or more important than his? Similar discussions did not seem to bother these men when they were with a woman of a different generation. They could allow an older woman to be more successful. They even expected it—but with women their own age, all kinds of hostilities erupted.

Dr. Michael Carrera, chairman of the board of the Sex Information and Education Council of the United States, believes that the younger man often finds the older woman more supportive of his particular needs and wants. She may make him feel more of a star in his own right. He knows she isn't going to compete with him. She's with him because she believes him special. She's interested in him for who he is.

Philip, 32, a clinical therapist who has been married for the past nine years to a woman thirteen years his senior and has adopted her ten-year-old child as his own, perhaps said it best: "There is no intrinsic reason why an older-woman/younger-man relationship is bound to either succeed or fail. It certainly is not any riskier than any other kind of intimate relationship. Relationships can end up failing for so many reasons. All too often, people look to their intimate relationships for solutions to a wide variety of personal problems, which only compound the difficulties in achieving true intimacy. If, on the other hand, two people are sure of themselves as individuals, if they know who they are or want to be, and they are compatible—which is always the basic consideration—then there is no reason at all why the relationship can't work even though the woman may be older. It is vital to remember, though, that the relationship itself can't solve any problems. If a woman is trying to recapture the lost flush of youth or if the man is trying to find a short cut to a more mature world or trying even to avoid growing up at all by finding a mother figure to depend on, there is likely to be disappointment. If both partners are mature individuals and respect each other as such, and if the age difference is only incidental and does not dominate the structure of the relationship, an older woman and a younger man can be very happy together. Great personal strength is not a prerequisite, nor is self-respect; rather, the man and the woman must respect each other. With love and mutual respect, intimacy is worth the gamble at any age. One of the nicest things about age differences is that it gets relatively smaller as time passes."

To that we say, "Amen."

3

THE WOMEN SPEAK

After conducting interviews with seventy-six women and mailing out questionnaires to numerous others, we held a discussion with twelve women who we felt best represented an interesting and varied sampling. The women's ages ranged from the early thirties to the late fifties. All but one (Fran) had been married and had children. Each was presently involved, in a relationship of some duration and significance, with a man at least seven years younger than she.

It was a cold, rainy Saturday afternoon, typical April in New York. Inside a midtown high-rise the comments were fast and furious. The questions and responses shot back and forth, cascading, ricocheting, bouncing from one to another. It was a consciousness-raising session for all involved. The subject was not one that had been covered in any feminist manifesto, though in many cases it appeared to be a direct by-product. The women began the afternoon as strangers. They left, many hours later, friends.

To the following we would like to offer our grateful and heartfelt thanks:

Jeanne, 37, who lives with Alan, 30;
Penny, 42, who is married to John, 23;
Ina, 39, who lives with Carl, 29;
Fran, 35, who lives with Wally, 25;
Nancy, 46, who is involved with Steve, 26;

Helen, 44, who lives with Marc, 24;
Vivian, 55, who lives with Ned, 45;
Alice, 52, who is involved with Robert, 38;
Hilda, 56, who is involved with Barry, 45;
Margo, 45, who is living with George, 23;
Laura, 33, who is living with Tom, 22;
Barbara, 48, who is involved with Frank, 26.

These women came together because they wanted to talk about and share similar experiences in order to help themselves and others understand the special problems and special joys that can come from their reverse May-December relationships. They seemed motivated by a need to reach out, to disclose, to find out about others involved in similar situations. There was no need to make up or distort; they were individuals bound by a common tie. In order to protect identities, we've altered descriptions and changed circumstances, but the words are the participants' own, taken from both the round-table discussion and the detailed questionnaires.

The day before we held this meeting, we had interviewed a highly successful and articulate professional woman who had discussed with us her own live-in relationship of twelve years with a man twenty-two years her junior. She confessed to us that in the beginning she had felt very uncomfortable whenever they went out. She thought people were saying, "What's that handsome man doing with that old lady?" When she finally found the courage to confess her thoughts, her lover's response was to stroke her cheek and say, "That's funny. If people are talking, and I don't think they are, they're probably saying, 'What's that good-looking, educated, developed person doing with the callow youth? What does she need him for?' What we're having is a May-December romance. The question is which of us is May and which of us is December."

As we looked at the group of alert, attractive faces seated about the room, we wondered if they'd shared a similar episode. Was it possible that they also had wondered, at some point in their relationship, which was May and which was December?

Alvin Toffler has written that minorities experiment, while majorities cling to the past. What will count, Dr. Toffler believes, will no longer be chronological age but, rather, complementary values and interests and, above all, the levels of personal development. He says partners will be interested in stage rather than age.[1]

Turning on the tape recorder, we allowed the women to speak for themselves. We posed our first question:

WHAT IS IT LIKE, BEING PART OF AN OLDER-WOMAN/YOUNGER-MAN RELATIONSHIP?

Fran, an unmarried literary agent of thirty-five with brown, shoulder-length hair parted in the middle and expressive hazel eyes that danced when she spoke, responded first.

"The answer is that it's great. Men my age or older don't appeal to me. Never have. Older men aren't into things the way younger men are. They're not as open to new thoughts and ideas. Nor are they struggling as I and most of my friends are to change our lives. When I'm with someone who's older than I am, I feel as if he's just looking for the moment when he can assert himself and take charge, and that scares me. I also feel that a man my own age isn't as interested in my career as he wants me to be with his. He isn't at all concerned about my business conflicts and successes but would much rather we focused on his problems. I get the feeling from these men that they think I'm trying to compete with them on what they consider their own turf, and with Wally, the man I'm living with, there's nothing like that taking place. I don't like a man playing Big Daddy. I want a man who knows who he is.

"Wally's twenty-five, a lawyer with Legal Aid who's involved in all kinds of causes and happenings. He's alive and vibrant and has a curiosity about life and people that turns me on and challenges me to try and keep up with him; to try and do as much as he does. He also believes in me. My career is as important to him as his is. An older man makes me want to rebel. I get the feeling of a 'Father Knows Best.' With Wally I can be myself. And when we're together there is no age difference."

Nancy, forty-six, a fair-skinned, tall, red-haired, successful management consultant to several large corporations, responded to Fran's remarks. Nancy had been married for fifteen years, divorced for eleven, and had two daughters, one age twenty-two, presently in graduate school, and the other twenty-five, living in California. Steve, the man's she's lived with on and off the past few years, is an aspiring writer of twenty-six.

"I feel the same way as you do, Fran. I've worked very hard to achieve my position in the business world and I have a very low tolerance for any man who considers himself my protector. In fact, I have no tolerance at all; it infuriates me. I'm not looking for a throwback; it interferes with my own independence. Besides, why should we hesitate to take on something that has been the prerogative of successful men for centuries just because it's never been an ordinary part of our culture for women to avail themselves of the same privileges that men have? All I know is that when we get behind closed doors I'm a woman and he's my man and that's the way it is.

"I have to admit, though, that falling in love with Steve was not part of my plans. What I wanted was to seduce him, to make love to him. I simply couldn't stand the fact that, because of my age, I was out of the running for a twenty-six-year-old I was extremely attracted to. It made me feel old and sexless and I couldn't bear it. When Steve said to me one night, many months later, that he'd never expected to fall in love with a woman old enough to be his mother, I told him that was all right—I hadn't expected to fall in love with a man young enough to be my son."

Helen, a slim, sun-bronzed woman with streaked blond hair and a voluptuous, graceful figure, smiled to herself as Nancy spoke. It was a smile of recognition. Three years ago, at the age of forty-one, Helen had packed a small suitcase. Taking only her essentials, she left an alcoholic husband of twenty-three years, an expensive home in the suburbs, all the material comforts anybody could want, and three children: two daughters in college and a son in boarding school. She didn't ask for, nor did she receive, a penny in alimony. She left because she was tired of the fighting and she didn't want to continue tilting at windmills. She said to herself: "You're forty years old. Isn't it time you stopped rehashing your past and living your life waiting for tomorrow?" So, taking advantage of artistic talents that previously had been categorized as "Sunday fiddling," she set up shop in a studio apartment in the city as a free-lance illustrator. Helen left her husband because, in her own words, she wanted to be happy. For the past three years, living with Marc, a graduate student by day, a waiter at night, a man twenty years her junior, she believes she has achieved her goal.

"Marc is a tender man with intense feelings. He's the warmest, most loving person I have ever encountered. I've never felt this way about any other man. But there is a Catch-22. I've become overly self-conscious about my age. When someone asks me how old I am, or when I have to fill my age out on an application blank, my hand starts to shake. I actually feel myself choking. I know I look young, and for damn sure I think young, but forty-four sounds to me like an old lady. I want to bury that number. I want to scream I'm not that person. I feel the same now as I did when I was twenty, maybe even better. But when I look at Marc and then at my-self, I know that one of us is playing 'Let's Pretend.'"

Vivian nodded. "Helen," she responded, "we all play that same game to some extent. (Vivian was fifty-five years old, a pleasant, gray-haired, stylishly dressed lawyer who lived with another lawyer, ten years her junior.)

"After four years of living together, I still haven't lost the feeling that one morning Ned's going to look at me across the breakfast table and see me as I really am and wonder what he's doing living with such an old person. Ned's forty-four, young enough to have and want a family of his own. I have my children, but Ned was divorced over ten years ago and never had any kids. Part of me feels great guilt—as if I'm keeping him from having a normal relationship. When-ever I see an older woman walking arm in arm with a younger man in the street, something clicks in my head and screams, 'Vivian, can't you see it? That's you. There's something wrong with this kind of relationship. There's something per-verted about it. . . .' Instead of feeling a kinship with the other woman, I grow embarrassed."

"I don't feel that way at all," Fran interrupted. "It's not fair that a man should be allowed so many more options than a woman. Why should everybody approve when the man is older and then, when the situation is reversed, society points its finger and shouts: 'Naughty, naughty! What are you doing? Who do you think you are?'—As far as I'm con-cerned we're all free to pick and choose whatever kind of relationship we want. Vivian, if the situation was reversed, if Ned was fifty-five and you were forty-four you'd probably say, 'Great.' Perfectly normal, average age difference. And as far as feeling bad about your keeping him from having children, I'm sure that's your hang-up, not his."

Jeanne, a brown-haired, blue-eyed, thirty-seven-year-old housewife who had arrived with a copy of *The Hite Report* under her arm spoke up next. (Jeanne lived in suburbia with her three children in the same home she'd occupied before splitting with her husband of thirteen years, a banker she described as ultraconservative. She has lived with Alan, age thirty, for three years.) "I'd like," Jeanne said, "to read aloud the following passage from this book, because it describes what happened to me. It's about an older-woman/younger-man relationship, a forty-three-year-old woman talking about her marriage and subsequent affair with a twenty-three-year-old.

" 'I was a frigid wife and became one as a result of the necessity of faking orgasms for the sake of preserving love. This wasn't because of my attitude toward the function of sex, but rather in a futile attempt to subordinate my own natural feelings to my husband's social conditioning. . . .[2] The first time I went to my lover I was terrified that I wouldn't be able to feel anything with him either. But he was so patient and skillful that I was able to rediscover what I had known so long before. He rewoke what I'd wasted so many years trying to deny. . . .[3]

"That describes me before I met Alan. It describes my marriage and how I felt. Alan's helped me to rediscover a part that I was afraid had died. He's helping me find the young Jeanne, and I love sharing her with him. I feel as if all of me has just come out of the closet. My mother's reaction when she first met Alan was, and I quote, 'You sure do like them young, don't you?' And that was after I'd added a couple of years to his age just to pacify her. What I was forgetting was my mother's conditioning. In her eyes, anyone a day younger is to be considered out of the running for my affections. What she doesn't understand is that Alan's made me feel like a kid. If anyone's the older, it's him, not me."

Alice smiled. "I don't know when I first fell in love with Robert," she said softly. (Alice was a gray-haired, carefully made up and elegantly dressed and coiffed fifty-two-year-old public-relations executive who had been widowed at the age of forty-eight, after twenty-five years of marriage. She had three children; the eldest daughter was thirty-three, five years younger than Robert, the advertising executive she was living with.)

"For me," Alice said, "ours was a very natural liaison. It didn't seem to matter that I'd been married and Robert hadn't. Or even that I had three children, my oldest daughter almost his age. We felt like peers, not a man and a woman who were fourteen years apart. The chemistry was very strong between us and the feeling was of love. A very deep love. We'd discussed age before any physical contact was made, and Robert made me feel as though age played no part in a relationship between a man and a woman. Feelings were what counted, he said. And they were either there or they weren't. I knew him a long while before any sexual relationship was initiated. When it came time for that component to be added, I wasn't at all self-conscious. To me, my body is like the weather—it's always with me. I accept it and enjoy it for what it is. We're very comfortable together. Age wasn't referred to at all when we made love the first time. Love-making gives one a sense of equality. It seemed to reduce any differences between us."

WHAT ATTRACTED YOU TO YOUR LOVER INITIALLY?

Nancy laughed. "I can give you all kinds of answers and spice it with psychological jargon, but if you want to know the truth, the answer is very concise. Initially, it was his body. Quite honestly, Steve is one of the best-looking men I've ever seen. I've always been attracted to beauty, and I find young men, with their taut, firm bodies, simply better-looking in every way. In addition, it struck me at the time—and it still does—that this was an act equivalent to that of an older man and a younger woman. Only, this time, I had the power and money, he the youth and beauty. I thought it an absolutely unique opportunity to find out how men felt trying to make it with girls who were inaccessible. Steve is a struggling writer. In a way, he's an innocent. He still has his faith, he believes in everything. He's sweet and vulnerable and there are times I've felt so much love for him that the sensation is actually painful."

Penny nodded. "It's hard for me to admit," she said, "but Nancy's answer about attraction is the same as mine." (Penny was a secretary in a small office who'd married at eighteen, had three children by the time she was twenty-two, and worked for sixteen of her twenty married years as a secretary to help support an alcoholic husband. She had recently married John, who was in the Navy, stationed overseas. She was planning to join him within the month.)

"John was nineteen when we first met. He was the son of a neighbor I didn't know well. One afternoon, he was outside washing his car. He was wearing tight-fitting pants and a tee shirt that accentuated every bicep. I thought: What a lean, hard body he has! From the first, I knew that I wanted to go to bed with him. If nothing else happened between us, I figured that would still be great. At that time, I was living with my husband, and you can believe me when I tell you that it was like beauty and the beast. My husband walked around in an undershirt—in an alcoholic stupor half the time. We hadn't had a decent sex life in years. I don't remember ever feeling as sexually attracted to a man as I felt with John, and after four years of being together, one of them married, I haven't lost any of that desire. But I am conscious of the difference in our looks. In a contest for the body beautiful, I'd lose hands down. John's tight and smooth, and no matter how I keep in shape there are sags where there shouldn't be and creases where I hate them. So I suppose what you're looking at is a woman who in her head still believes she's nineteen, but nowhere else. What can I do if my body lies?"

Margo, a striking, light-skinned, forty-five-year-old black woman, spoke for the first time. Margo's hair was pinned straight back in a French knot. She was tall and fine-boned. Her face was chiseled, and when she spoke, everything seemed to light up at once. (Margo had been married when she was twenty-three, divorced when she was thirty, and had a daughter a year older than George, the man she was living with.)

"I think," she said, "that what attracted me to George initially was the fact that he didn't seem to notice that I was there. That he seemed so very inaccessible. He was the outstanding student at the high school where I was in charge of the Drama Department, and on top of that he was extremely good-looking. I made up my mind I was going to seduce him when he turned eighteen, and I did. He was terrified and embarrassed and not at all sure it was a good idea for us to become lovers, though he admitted he was very attracted to me. I told him that it was all right, I valued his friendship, and added that if nothing further happened sexually between us, we would always be friends. Soon after we had this conversation, he called one night and asked if he could come over and discuss our possible relationship. If anyone had ever suggested to me before this happened that I would have an affair with a man half my age and end up living with him, in what has become one of my longer sustaining relationships (my marriage lasted seven years and this is going on five), I would have told them they were crazy—and demanded an apology. And I wouldn't have been satisfied until I received it."

WHAT WENT THROUGH YOUR MIND WHEN YOU UNDRESSED BEFORE YOUR LOVER FOR THE FIRST TIME?

Laura, a pert blond actress who had been married for seven years and had two children when she was divorced at thirty, responded first. (Laura had been married to a man six years older and had been in business with him, owning and operating a West Side New York clothing boutique. She'd studied acting and was supporting herself by making television commercials. For the past year, she's been living with Tom, a struggling and, more frequently than not, unemployed actor of twenty-two. Laura was thirty-three.)

"What went through my mind," Laura said, "was sheer pleasure. I stood up as straight as I could, hoping everything would hold up and stretch out. At the time, rather than attributing it to age, I blamed it on vanity. I've always been extremely conscious of my body. Just before the relationship with Tom began, I lost weight and felt very proud of myself. As a matter of fact, I was feeling so strongly about having an improved shape that I wanted to hear men say how nice it was . . . and not from a distance. From the time I was thirteen, I've hated my flat chest and fat thighs. Every time I would undress before a man, I would check my angles of vision and wish I could remake myself instantaneously—sort of in the image of Raquel Welch. I studied myself in the mirror, turning from side to side, examining my profile, wondering if I had a wrinkle where I shouldn't or that my breasts and tummy weren't as firm as a nineteen-year-old's. Tom thought he was complimenting me when he looked at me with admiration and said, 'You sure don't have middle-aged spread, do you?' At that moment, I felt every year that separated us. I wanted to say that people of all ages can be fat and being middle-aged has nothing to do with it. And that if my body looked good to him it was because it was in good shape and age was beside the point. You see, in my mind what he'd said was, 'You're old, Laura. You just look young.'"

"Remarks like that can be very painful," Barbara, a forty-eight-year-old vice-president of a career-consulting firm, remarked, "and they take a long time to forget." (Barbara had married at age twenty-five a man eighteen years older than she was. The marriage lasted fourteen years and she'd had two sons, both of whom lived away from home. She'd worked steadily from the age of thirty. Frank, the man she's been with the past two and one half years, is a photographer and twenty-six.)

"When Frank and I met, I considered my body to be in reasonably good shape, considering that I'd had two kids and by my own standard had passed rather serenely into middle age. I knew I wasn't as taut as I'd been twenty years ago and by no means did I have the shape of a twenty-year-old, but I liked what I saw when I looked in the mirror. Yet, the first time we made love, I was very conscious of my age. I remember taking my clothes off ever so carefully, holding as much of myself in as I could, waiting for Frank's reaction. You see, from the beginning, it's seemed to me that he's held the sexual power between us. I desire him more than he desires me. He's the tease, not I. Anyway, I was more aware than ever before of my every blemish, and I was very relieved when he reassured me that my body was good. Not until then did I lose some of my apprehension. There were four small moles on my middle that I hadn't thought about in years, but when we were making love I became very self-conscious about them. Frank asked me what the matter was, and when I pointed them out to him, he kissed each one as if to show that he loved them, also. It was the most tender gesture anybody had ever made toward me. I think I loved him from that point on."

Hilda, a plump, very petite, fifty-six-year-old high school English teacher, looked at Barbara with something akin to awe. (Hilda had been divorced, when she was in her late forties, from her college-math-professor husband. Her daughter and son were both in their twenties and unmarried. At the time of our discussion, Hilda was living in the same house as her sixty-year-old unmarried sister. Barry, the man she had been involved with for the past two and one half years, worked for the Post Office. He was forty-five.)

"I can't seem to get around the fact that I'm at least fifteen pounds overweight and feel that I must resemble a comfortable, somewhat overstuffed couch. The first time I undressed at Barry's apartment, it was black as the ace of spades in the room. All my negative feelings were aroused at fever pitch. At the same time, I felt myself more sexually attracted than I'd been for a very long time. My husband had been seven years older than I was and he had lost interest in sex years before we split. He'd told me, 'Sex means nothing. If you want it, you can have an affair, I don't care.' This I refused to do, and when Barry came along I was very apprehensive. I had a few other relationships, but he was the first man who was appreciably younger than I was. I was afraid he'd notice all my flab and wouldn't think I was a good lover. I was so self-conscious about all my sagging parts that if I could, I would have left my bra and girdle on. I had this fantasy that once he saw me nude I would give myself away. You see, I had lied about my age. And I didn't admit the truth until we were lovers for eight months, and then only because I was afraid someone else would tell him. When I finally confessed, Barry's reaction really surprised me. He thought it was funny. Said it didn't change his feelings or regard for me a bit. It seems the pressures of differences in age were very one-sided."

WAS SEX A MAJOR PART OF YOUR RELATIONSHIP
AND WAS IT DIFFERENT THAN WITH
LOVERS YOUR OWN AGE OR OLDER?

Ina, a tall, very well-endowed magazine writer of thirty-nine, recently divorced from her lawyer husband of sixteen years, shook her head no. (Ina had a teen-age daughter and two younger sons. She lived with Carl, age twenty-nine, a free-lance writer in New Jersey.)

"There are no age barriers when it comes to making love, at least not for me. When I make love to a man, it is to a totality and not to whatever age he may be. I'm more aggressive by nature, but Carl usually initiates our love-making. He's very powerful and dominant in sex, and I like feeling that he's taking charge in this area. It makes me feel more desirable, and there seems to be an equality between us. Carl is also intensely loving after making love, and that to me is very special. And such a contrast to my husband, who usually fell asleep thirty seconds after he was finished!

"I enjoy sex with Carl more than with any man I've ever known. It's been very important from the beginning. And I still feel this way after three years. Experimentation wasn't an important aspect of this. It's just been a matter of deeper and more-flowing feeling. I've always thought of sex as just a physical expression of love. The only difference is that with Carl it seems to encompass so many facets. It's both passionate and quiet, lustful and affectionate, and serious and playful. Loving and caring seem paramount in our relationship, and it makes the passion greater and the sex the most exciting I've ever had in my life."

Margo: I don't feel that way. While the sex with George has been very good, it seems to me that older lovers are more experienced and know more about a woman's body. The reason I enjoy it so much with George is due to something else: Lovers my age seem to want to prove something. They're intent on showing their own masculinity. George only wants to enjoy me.

When it began with George, I was the teacher in every sense of the word. Before me, George had only had one-night stands with girls his own age. He was only eighteen, which, I suppose from all I've read, is the height of a man's sexual powers, and he was very energetic and anxious to please. Much more so than any other man I've ever known. He was very warm and demonstrative, and there's always been lots of cuddling.

Before George, I had always taken a back seat sexually. I had just turned forty when this began, and it hit me that all my life, it's always been a man who has initiated sex. That's probably part of the reason I picked a man I wanted to seduce. You reach a certain stage when you want to be the aggressive one, when you want to do your own picking and choosing.

Laura: The first few times Tom and I made love, he appeared very insecure. Very much the young twenty-two-year-old. He had a lovely body and he was quite sexual, but he seemed anxious and much less experienced than any other man I'd ever been with. We enjoyed each other thoroughly in bed and still do, but we've never been able to talk there. If I should mention anything that I'd like to try or do, it turns him off. As if I'm threatening his masculinity or what he feels should be his instinctive knowledge. Still, our love-making has always been very tender, and I often feel as if I'm taking care of him. Afterward, we both feel like a couple of kids.

Barbara: Sex is a mystical symbiosis for me, and no two relationships are anything alike. It certainly has nothing to do with age. I've never had a lover who made me feel he was like another. Each relationship has its own content, largely undefinable and I don't think describable. Frank's an ex-Catholic, and he has retained a certain sense of sin about sex, which is sometimes frustrating and other times piquant and exotic. He doesn't talk during love-making and I like pillow talk, but he is very passionate. The strange thing is I've had lovers not much older than Frank and I have not been that conscious of their age, but between us the feeling's always there. It's not age that causes it but an attitude—his attitude that what we're doing with one another is not quite right.

Helen: Marc was very apprehensive that first time, and though he'd told me he found me very attractive, he was afraid that sex would complicate everything and we might no longer be friends. I think he was embarrassed and nervous about our getting together sexually, and I understood his feelings, because I felt a great many of them too. Maybe even more than he, but I didn't verbalize. Anyway, it seemed to me that he was waiting for me to take charge of the situation. For me to come on to him, and I suppose that's what happened. He's since confessed that he likes to think of me as worldly. He likes it when I do the seducing; it fits his image of me as a woman of vast experience. And it makes me feel sexier than I ever have before.

Penny: Sex became very important in our relationship once John and I were able to face it. In the beginning, I tried to repress my feelings. I was afraid he'd think me a cradle robber. . . . Don't forget this was the kid across the street with a mother who was around my age. Not to mention the fact that I was still married at the time. So, though I wanted to have sex with him from the moment I saw him outside that afternoon, our relationship was nonsexual for the first few dates. When he showed that he found me as attractive as I felt him to be, I became less inhibited and took the sexual initiative, acting out my feelings.

John had this image of me as a woman of the world, and that seemed to turn him on. He appeared to get a kick out of what he termed my "experience." Later he told me that he was concerned about being a good lover and giving me as much pleasure as I was used to. The sad fact was that with my husband I wasn't used to anything. Anyway, our lovemaking has always been very passionate. Since John seems so appreciative of everything about me, I've become more turned on to myself, and what I've found is that I have a great amount of love to give.

WHAT WERE THE REACTIONS OF YOUR PEERS?

Fran: I try my best not to dwell on other people's reactions. I always do what I think is best for me. If friends understood me, I felt they would understand the relationship, and most of the people that I know didn't seem very surprised. I almost think, rather than wondering about it in depth, they felt lots of women were into a younger-man relationship for a fling, the only way they could relate to it. Many of these same friends remarked they thought it was cute, and that sentiment more than anything else drove me up the wall.

Wally's very involved in social causes and we usually mix with the people he's working with. We don't discuss our relationship with anyone except ourselves, and we tend to ignore comments if there are any. At a party at our house recently, I looked around the room and realized I was the only one there over thirty. This gave me a start; I had a very funny feeling for a few minutes, but it passed. Everyone seemed very accepting, and even if they weren't I feel that that's their problem, not mine.

Barbara: My peers thought I was bananas and so I avoided explaining anything to them. I am too old for explanations anyway, and it hadn't bothered me as much as it bothered Frank when some of his friends reacted similarly. Two women friends with whom I've been particularly close over the years thought it was a turn-on. Said it opened their minds to new ideas about possible relationships. I was glad of that, but I also felt that even these women didn't take what was happening in my life seriously. I felt most of my friends were condescending, the women more so than the men. They patronized Frank by saying things like: "You wouldn't re-

member that, you're way too young." "It's before your time."
Et cetera.

The general feeling I came away with from my peers was
that my affair was okay for a fling, maybe even better than
okay, but if I was intent on taking it seriously, I was in for a
pile of trouble.

Jeanne: I've had just the opposite reaction. Everyone I
care about has been very supportive of Alan and myself from
the beginning. They liked him, and when they saw he made
me happy, that was good enough for them. As a matter of
fact, Alan has a beard, which makes him look older, so in the
beginning no one was conscious that there was much of a
difference between us. But I was very self-conscious. When-
ever we went out with someone, I would make it a point to
refer to the fact that Alan was still in graduate school and had
a lot of catching up to do until he was as old as I was. That
has since stopped, and now we never refer to the difference
in our ages.

The only time my friends expressed doubts was when I
told them we planned on marrying, once Alan gets his degree.
They became wary and suggested I should be satisfied with
the status quo. They knew that Alan wanted his own children
and felt that I was letting myself in for more than I could
handle. I told them I appreciated their concern, but what
Alan wants is what I want; in fact I planned on becoming
pregnant immediately after we married. I stretched the truth
here a bit; I can't say having another baby excites me at this
point in my life, but I think what Alan's asking is fair, and
how can I deny him a child of his own?—In a way, I suppose
my friends share some of my own worries; only, they ver-
balized them and I never have . . . until this afternoon.

Alice: The reaction of my peers was mixed: horror, envy,
curiosity; I suppose a little bit of everything. But always
belittling and negating, constantly warning that Robert will

never stay with me, because of our large age difference. As if I or they believed in forever anyway. It never seems to enter their heads that in terms of staying power this relationship has lasted much longer than many of their more "conventional" ones. . . . In any event, the reactions never seem to be in between. Whatever else this relationship provokes, it is not indifference. Everyone seems to have a definite opinion on it, and none of these opinions seem to take into account the people involved. In other words, I don't feel my friends are weighing Robert's and my feelings about one another. They act as if feelings are incidental, not crucial, to what's at stake. I feel that we're crossing some very delicate social taboo.

It's taken a long time to weigh the objections and comments from all sources and to decide that nothing could or should stand in the way of what are our own feelings. We've been together over two years now, and while those closest to us pretend to understand, I don't believe they do. . . . Or in fact ever will. And I would like to echo what Barbara said before. My men friends and male business associates have been, on the whole, much more affirmative than the women. And I wish I could understand the reasons for this.

IF YOU HAD CHILDREN FROM A PREVIOUS
MARRIAGE, DID THEY ACCEPT
YOUR RELATIONSHIP
OR DID THEY TRY TO EXPLOIT
THE AGE DIFFERENCE?

Vivian: Publicly my children accept the age difference between Ned and myself. We've gone out together and they've spent weekends with us both. They appear glad that I'm happy, but in private my oldest daughter told me she wished I was a little more down to earth. That she doesn't regard this as an average relationship—whatever that means. And yet she likes Ned very much and is very pleasant toward him. Once, when we were all out together, she met a friend and introduced Ned as her stepfather. I was surprised she did this, but pleased. I felt as if she was trying the idea out for size. She's never tried to talk me out of the relationship, and most of the time she maintains a polite distance. Since I know how my children feel, I don't see them as often as I might otherwise, and when I do, I'm not as comfortable around them as I would ordinarily be.

Margo: My daughter reacted very negatively in the beginning. Her attitude affected me greatly, to the point where I almost allowed it to destroy the relationship between George and myself. And this was when I was already in love with him. She had been only a year ahead of George in high school, and one of her friends had dated him before we got together. How could I blame her for being in a state of confusion and pain? There seemed to be so many things going on that I didn't think any of us would survive intact.

The most important thing I did was not to allow her to make me ashamed of my feelings and to show her that I really did care for George, no matter what happened to the romance. Her immediate reaction was to move out of the house and to take an apartment with a friend. A week later, George moved in. When she moved out, the tension eased, and even though it took a while, she's become fairly accepting. She sees that we're happy together and that we genuinely care about and for one another. The other day, she remarked she couldn't remember ever seeing me as relaxed and young-looking, and then she went so far as to offer that George and I must be doing something right. I smiled and said we were, and she gave me a kiss on the cheek and said she was glad. Life became much easier for us all when I left my job at the high school and accepted one at the college where George is now getting his MBA.

Hilda: I have a son twenty-six and a daughter almost thirty. They are very disapproving on all counts. They don't approve of the age difference, nor do they like what they perceive as a class difference, of what they call our backgrounds. They make it very clear that they don't want to be in Barry's presence. It's interesting, because they never made their feelings vocal when their father tried to keep me tied to the house, denying me any rights whatsoever. That was legitimate in my kids' eyes, but this relationship, to them, even though it makes me happy, is a total disaster. When we are all together, they're openly hostile, so I try to keep our lives separate.

Funny thing is that this bothers me more than it bothers Barry. His family has been very supportive and warm toward me. They've never made me feel "too old." I don't know if they even know how old I am.

Ina: My oldest daughter was eleven when Carl moved in. She was and still is embarrassed by the situation. I have two younger boys and they're both openly affectionate toward Carl, but they're only seven and nine, and they react toward him as if he were their friend. What they like about Carl more than anything is his willingness to play ball with them, to take them to sporting events; things that their father isn't mad about doing.

My daughter is at the stage where it's difficult for her to accept anybody, probably even herself. We live in the suburbs, and not only have I flaunted convention by living with a man ten years younger, but the very fact that I'm living with a man at all who's not my husband is frowned upon by most of my neighbors.

Of course, my daughter's attitude affects us; how could it not, when we're all under one roof? For the past few months, she and I have been going to a therapist together, and that has helped ease the tension considerably. But what's helped most of all is that my kids see that Carl and I are respectful toward one another and that this is a stable relationship, with some permanence about it. The fact that we're still together after three years has reassured them more than anything else.

Laura: My kids are too young to recognize any age differences. The only thing that concerned them was that Tom appeared to be taking me away from their father. I met him right after my divorce, and when he moved in, the kids figured I was bringing them another daddy, and they didn't like this, because they were very attached to the one they already had.

Tom was crazy about the boys. When they rejected him at any time, for whatever reason, he would become depressed. He's just a year out of his mother's house, and when the boys acted up, he sometimes suggested I go back to my husband. I would get very angry with him when he reacted this way, and we'd end up hassling, with my telling him he's acting as big a baby as my kids and his telling me he's leaving me because I'm too old for him.

Barbara: I've never discussed any of my relationships with my sons. The oldest is twenty-seven, a year older than Frank, and he lives out West. My youngest is in law school. If either of them comes home for a few days, Frank moves into the guest room, and he's very careful that there's never a hint of physical affection between us. He's very self-conscious about the fact that I have kids approximately his age, and he doesn't like seeing me function in the mother-son role. It just so happens this is fine with me; I know that if he was more overt or obvious, I would be the one backing off. It's not that I'm trying to conceal myself as a sexual person in front of my children, it's just that I believe in privacy and I'm not looking to hold my life up to inspection. My sons know that we're lovers, but it's my thing, not theirs. And that's the way I want it to be.

ARE YOU INVOLVED WITH
EACH OTHER'S BUSINESS CAREER?

Nancy: I've never permitted my business and social life to
overlap. I don't like it when a man does it; I try not to do it
either. I prefer to go to all meetings, even conventions, alone
or with professional colleagues. There's much less hassle, and
I think it's boring for people not directly involved. I did this
when I was married, too, so I'm certainly not singling Steve
out because of his age. He's pretty much unemployed much
of the time, so there isn't any business-connected social life
for him. Strike that—he's not unemployed, he just hasn't
been recognized as the fine writer that he is. I'm sure that recognition won't be too far off.

Last summer, I was away in California for over a month on
business and also visiting my daughter, and I missed him terribly. And I think, deep down, I wanted my daughter to meet
him. To see how wonderful he was. I offered to wire him the
fare and pleaded with him to come, but he refused—I pre-
sume on the grounds that he didn't want to accept the
money. He has strict ground rules on accepting more than he
can afford to pay back, but, of course, I can't be sure this was
the reason.

Ina: Carl and I work for two separate magazines housed in
the same office building, and this is a big plus in our relationship. It also gives us a lot of alone time, away from everybody, on the ride to and from the city. Initially, I worried
that Carl's colleagues would give him a hard time and try to
talk him out of it and question him why he was interested in
a woman who was not only older but had three kids. The
funny thing is I never worried about my own co-workers' response. I figured they knew me and realized that this was a serious relationship for me and that I expected it to be taken

that way by others. I suppose I was more worried about Carl's peers because I was afraid of being stereotyped, but as it's turned out, all our co-workers have been very supportive and we've ended up socializing at night with the people that we see during the day. I think sharing friends in common is a great plus in our relationship, and I believe, regardless of age, it helps to work at similar jobs, because you have greater understanding of the other person's problems and tensions.

Vivian: I agree with you, Ina. When you're part of the same profession you also have many of the same shared perceptions. Ned and I work for large law firms down in Wall Street. We often find ourselves on the phone during the day discussing and sharing a legal problem, and I think we've been equally encouraging and supportive of each other's career. Ned verbalizes more about his work problems than I do and he's constantly asking me how I would handle this or that case. And I find I like being included in this aspect of his life. I've become much more emotionally involved in his work than he has with mine, but only because I have more of a tendency to try and work things out alone. We socialize with colleagues from both offices, but I think his friends have become more mine, rather than the other way around. There was only one co-worker that I know of who made a comment about our age difference. Ned was playing tennis with a partner I had met the previous evening. The man remarked he hadn't realized I was as old as I was. He wasn't trying to be cruel, at least Ned didn't think so, it was more in the nature of an observation, and so, rather than respond, Ned just nodded and let it pass.

CAN AGE BE FORGOTTEN IN
A SUCCESSFUL, ONGOING RELATIONSHIP?

Alice: The only reason I believe age is a factor at all is because one or both partners lack confidence in themselves. Age can only be an issue when you allow it to be. When you're sure of yourself and your feelings, there's no reason why you can't forget the numbers and think of yourself as this person. This woman who happens to care about this man. Loving Robert has caused me to change my entire outlook on my life and the people in it. I've learned a great deal about myself. I now feel I have much more courage to say the things I feel and do what I believe in but was never able to acknowledge before. Robert's made me feel sexier than anyone ever has. I think I actually became more so because of his feelings. What happened is that his youth has extended mine. Imagine feeling sexier at fifty-two than you ever have in your life. What can I tell you except that it's lovely? And so completely unexpected. It is a gift.

Jeanne: Well, I'm not as sanguine as you are, Alice. It's true that age doesn't play much of a part in Alan's and my daily life, but it looms monstrously large for me when I dwell on the future. I can't tuck it away, no matter how much I'd like to. After two years of living together, this is still the key question for me. What will it be like for us in ten or fifteen years? I'm not any closer to resolving it or reconciling my fears. It seems to sit out there, on the fringe, coloring my future, waiting, even though I try to brush it aside. It always appears most obvious when I'm feeling my lowest, on the days when everything else seems to be falling apart, so why not that? I've discussed this briefly with Alan and he's tried to reassure me. Most times, he succeeds; after all, Alan and I plan on marrying next year, but as for age being completely forgotten, the answer is no. In the long run, there's too much to remind you of it.

Helen: I feel the same way. Growing older frightens me; it always has. And being with a younger man accentuates that fear rather than alleviating it. It's not today I worry about, but what will I be like in ten years? I'm forty-four now and in pretty good shape. I exercise fairly regularly, and my muscles are strong and well toned. Marc's constantly telling me how attractive I am. But he's only twenty-four. I can't compete with a woman his age in the department of looks, and I can't help being aware that he's much more desirable to women than I am to men at this stage of my life. I suppose I've always equated good looks with power in the sexual marketplace, and this is what aging represents to me: the loss of my eligibility. Marc keeps telling me I'm silly, because he's not attracted to young girls, but it's an emotional response I can't control. I love him, but I'm sure the relationship will end soon. The age difference is too great and it can't be forgotten, just as you can't forget other things that aren't equal. When I think of Marc I don't just think that's the man I love but, rather, that's the *young* man I love.

Vivian: Not only do I not think age can be forgotten, I don't believe that it should be forgotten. My age is what makes me me. It's my experience, and I know it's what attracted Ned to me in the first place. It so happens I'm a much more attractive and interesting person now than I was ten, even twenty, years ago. When I was younger, I used to fly off the handle over anything and everything. I think the ability not to be angry over small things only comes with age. So does tolerance. When you're older, you know that not only can't the relationship last forever but, much more important, you're not going to last forever. So instead of carrying on, you just relax and enjoy. We've all heard age is only a number and I think that's true, it's only real on your birth certificate. If you're going to sit around and worry because society says that, at such and such an age, you are not supposed to act in such and such a way, well, then, you are letting society dictate your life. I've had one life before this—and three terrific children, a twenty-three-year-old marriage, and a law degree came out of it. Now I feel as if I'm continuing on but veering off in another direction. Maybe age is the sum total of everything.

Inside, I feel the same as I did when I was twenty—but, you know something, I'm a hell of a lot smarter and more with-it now and I'm not going to deny or negate that. I've told you that I'm not especially enamored about the physical part of growing old. Who is? But I can't erase my wrinkles and creases or negate where they come from. And I'm going to confess something else: I have the sneaking suspicion that if, for some unforeseen reason, Ned and I should break up to-morrow, I will still be interested in men who are younger. They just have more vitality and I think we offer each other more emotional security. I'm resolved never to let age stand in the way of the whole person.

Nancy: I feel much the same. Something that exists and looms as large as age can't be tucked away, especially when there's such a large difference as between Steve and myself. It seems to me that what happens is that you usually meet each other halfway. In a sense, Steve knows more about me than any other man. I think this is because, from the begin-ning, I never considered this to be an end-all relationship. I've told him a great deal more about myself than I would ever tell a man on whom I might have a "design for perma-nence." Steve is my lover and friend of my spirit. He pleases me by being beautiful and sensitive and by just being. He doesn't expect me to be part of the "Pepsi Generation," and I don't ask him to be more settled than it's possible for him to be. I know that at times I've been taken for Steve's mother, and that embarrasses and infuriates me, but there's not much I can do about it. Other times, it's seemed to me that my life is Steve's nostalgia, but when it comes down to it, this is all beside the point. I refuse to be placed into a category based on my age, nor will I let society tell me what is or isn't the proper thing to do. I've never pretended to be everywoman. Not at twenty, not now.

In the beginning, I thought Steve liked the made-up look

and I wouldn't go anywhere without looking all together. And then, one day, he told me he didn't like the makeup and that ended that. I've always dressed fairly youthful, and I did change my hair style at his request. Because of him, and with him, I feel I can act as young or as old as I want. He's got such vitality, such energy. And best of all, I don't threaten him, we don't compete in any way—except maybe one: I'll never get used to the idea that I am not utterly and tormentingly sexually desirable, as desirable as Steve is, and that every man should lust after me.

I have had relationships with other younger men but none have lasted as long as Steve or loomed so large in my life. And the unusual part of this is that the age difference between Steve and myself is the greatest of any man I've been with; too great, I believe, to ever think of permanence. And this isn't just due to years, it's also due to the vast differences in our life-styles, in our social backgrounds and experiences. That's why I don't believe age can ever be forgotten—when because of it so much else separates you.

ARE THERE ANY SPECIAL FEARS OR
PITFALLS INHERENT TO THIS TYPE
OF RELATIONSHIP?

Jeanne: Definitely. In every relationship, there are insecurities, but in this type they seem to be heightened. If you have any anxieties about your attractiveness, they usually take on even stronger overtones. You know, the man, if only because of his youth, is considered more sexually attractive than you are and there's nothing you can do about it. Even good friends make you wary at times with well-meaning remarks such as: "You look so young and Alan really looks much older than he is. It's hard to tell there's any difference between you."

As kind as these remarks are meant to be, you know that people are still trying to equalize the age difference in their heads and you begin to wonder how long you can keep it up. Will it always be so easy? What about next year? And the year after? You're vulnerable not only to what your man thinks and the way he sees you but also to the way you're viewed by both your peers and his. I hate it when friends give me a piece of well-meaning advice about staying fit. I take it personally, even when it's meant in the very broadest sense. But it activates my paranoia—I feel as if they're giving me a warning about the future in the subtlest way. So what I try to watch out for more than anything else is not to let other people's reactions, and my reactions to what I feel they're saying, affect me so much that they destroy what I now have.

Nancy: You also have to guard against the feeling that because the man is younger than you are, you bear a great deal of the responsibility for his future. Maybe it's a maternal feeling of sorts, I don't know. But I don't think I demand as much from a man younger than myself. On the other hand, I demand all kinds of things from someone my own age or older. I know there's no way Steve is going to be able to support my emotional needs. Nobody can be everything to anybody. When one partner has had many more life experiences than the other, often understanding of the opposite one's feelings is limited. Steve has had trouble socially with my contemporaries, and rather than fall into the trap of arguing over friends, we play the issue down. By virtue of his age alone, he hasn't had the time or success to acquire the polish or sense of security many of my peers have, who are, for the most part, very career-oriented men and women. That's why we're very careful to allow each other breathing room, and we don't demand more than the other can give. I think that's the reason we've lasted this long. That and the fact that our energy levels are the same in spite of the age difference. Otherwise, I know I would be exhausted half the time.

Helen: I try not to think of Marc and myself in terms of permanence, because in my gut I also believe that twenty years is much too large an age difference and it doesn't matter here if the man is older or the woman. I've gone through my crazy period worrying what will happen when I'm sixty and he's forty, seventy and fifty, and that's finally past. I realize that what I was looking for was just reassurance that he'd be in my life forever even though I no longer know what that word means.

When I finally broke away from all I'd known, I wasn't looking to be any kind of pioneer. When Marc moved in, we both agreed it was only temporary. To test the waters, so to speak, and we were both looking to cut down expenses, neither of us having much of an income. We figured two could live cheaper than one. The problem is we've been together almost three years now and it's no longer so easy to rationalize. There'll come a time when Marc will leave, he'll have to for his own well-being. He'll want to start a life with someone more his contemporary and maybe have a family or whatever. And while part of me says he would be right to do so, that it would be healthier both for him and for me, another part says, "Helen, you love him—you may not be strong enough to let him go!" . . . I want him to move out and I want him to stay. I'm afraid that one day he'll look at me and I'll be old and wrinkled and who'll want me then? It's not growing older, it's looking older, that's my nightmare.

Hilda: I share much the same fears that have been expressed. For me there's constant worry about appearance and also about becoming an overprotective or surrogate mama. I've learned a great deal from being with a man younger than I am. I feel most secure when I'm acting maternal. I suppose because I feel as if I'm in command. And being in command means worrying about what Barry's going to eat, taking care of him when he's ill, and being able to console and listen to what sometimes seems like a crisis a day. I worried about this in the initial stages of our relationship. I thought I'd have to break it off. But he seems to need that part of me and I like giving to him whatever I can.

I'm also very unnerved by other persons' comments. There are so many social pressures against older women and younger men that I have a fear of losing out in the value judgments of friends and immediate family. When Barry comes over to the house, my sister always makes clear her negative feelings and we very rarely stay there long. I suppose what it comes down to is a lack of trust on my part. A lack of self-esteem. A feeling deep down inside of me that it's really not okay for this relationship to survive. And that my friends and family are probably right when they negate it.

Barbara: The pitfall I try most to avoid is expecting too much of Frank—both in regard to what he is basically and, as Nancy mentioned before, in expecting him to fill all my needs. I have no hopes or expectations of Frank's ever being able to support me financially, nor would I want him to. Neither do I expect him to be completely faithful. I know that he sees women his own age from time to time, and strangely enough this doesn't scare me. I'd feel much more threatened if he'd found someone my own age to go out with, because even though the physical might be more exciting with a young woman, I feel that that doesn't last as long, and I really believe that I know more than the girls his age and that I have more to offer.

I don't want to make too many demands on Frank. That's the surest way to lose him. He is what he is. If I'd made demands, I would have gone down to defeat long ago. I'm afraid of wanting, of needing too much from him, and I am aware at all times that the most necessary thing for our relationship is that we provide one another enough space.

ARE THERE QUALITIES YOU FEEL
ARE UNIQUE TO AN OLDER-WOMAN/
YOUNGER-MAN RELATIONSHIP?

Alice: It is the most unusual relationship I've ever had in my life. Robert's a constant source of pleasure and delight to me. It's the first time in my life I have ever shared so much of myself with a man, and to have someone who understands what it is you're saying— that's a fabulous bonus. We've given each other a great deal and learned so much from being together. He's very open, and I know this is because of his age. He just hasn't had the chance to have been through as many bad relationships as the man who is my age peer. He believes in life and he has a spirit of adventure that's contagious. There's so much affection and love between us now that I feel he'll always be in my life, though I know we'll never marry. There'll come a time in the future when it will be right for him to marry someone younger so that he can have a family of his own and enjoy all the pleasures of the kind of life I can't give him. And when that time comes I'll still be there . . . on the outside, looking in.

I will tell you something else. This relationship has made me less conscious of my physical aging than any other I've had. I believe younger men don't notice wrinkles, pouches, whatever—as much as older men. I think the reason is because they don't have to worry about it. They have their own youth, so they're not looking to try and reclaim it. Because Robert acts and feels and enjoys being young, I do too, and the fact that I can forget about my age when I'm with him is, for me, one of the greatest pleasures of the relationship. He's my most extraordinary friend. He gives me the feeling that anything's possible.

Margo: It's true, Jeanne—everything you just said. George is the first man with whom I have not been afraid to share all the parts of myself. I don't know why, but with him the Huck Finn part of me comes out. He's the most affectionate, warmest person I've ever met. I'm basically a tomboy at heart and it's as if he's given me a license to let it all hang out. And I think it is because he doesn't have this role fixed in his head that says today you're supposed to do and be such and such. A younger man will never say to you, "Stop acting so silly; why don't you act your age?" There isn't any fixed age for either one of you; you're more or less captive of both worlds, and because the relationship is such an open one, there's no attempt to hide the differences. Instead you thrive on them. It's a constant giving.

When you're not competing on any level, the relationship is more honest. I know I don't have the fear of betrayal that usually comes when I'm with a man my age. I can tell George everything, because I'm not afraid. He appreciates me for what I am—and where I am in my life. I find this a very welcome attitude when I compare it to men of my generation, who are trying to turn back the clock and recapture their past, who refuse to be seen with any woman who might remind them that the years have a way of adding up. Since George has no self-consciousness about aging—mine or his—I often forget the generations that separate us. He thinks I'm young and I think I'm young and what's wrong with that? He helps me to be less afraid. Sometimes when I'm really feeling optimistic I think I'll be able to forget about the mirror once and for all. . . .

Another big advantage is that sex is a solved problem for me. His appetite matches mine. We're perfectly mated in this area, and I see no signs of that abating. We come from two different places, two different generations, but we're anxious to give our best to one another.

WHAT ADVICE WOULD YOU GIVE TO SOMEONE CONTEMPLATING AN OLDER-WOMAN/YOUNGER-MAN RELATIONSHIP?

Ina: I don't think people plan on falling in love. And when it happens, I don't believe age is a significant factor. For me, the most important thing is that my relationship with Carl differs from my marriage of sixteen years in that it is a loving and sharing one. I'm doing things that I always wanted to do before, like camping and hiking and sports. In my whole life I've never felt about sex as I do now. I always believed I had it in me to enjoy it fully, but it was always waiting for someone to bring it out. So what I'm saying is love is mysterious, and when it comes, with whomever it comes, you should feel very lucky. If anyone's contemplating an experience with a younger man, I would tell them: "Don't prejudge. Let whatever happens, happen. Accept each other for what you both are and not for what you would like each other to be. Be flexible and open and understanding of your own needs as well as his. He has come to you for a reason. Your need for him is perhaps for another reason. But that doesn't matter. Just relax and be yourself and enjoy both worlds. And don't ever lower or falsify your age, because if you accept it with all the ramifications, then you won't be that hurt if the affair ends. When you find yourself worrying about how long the relationship is going to last, think, if it lasts two years or five or ten, then that's two or five or ten years more happiness than you have had before. Say to yourself, "This is a new experience. I am going to enjoy every moment of it."

Vivian: I believe if someone is contemplating this kind of relationship, they should stop analyzing it and go ahead without paying undue attention to what society might say. Please yourself and, chances are, given the circumstances, sooner or later, these others will be right in there alongside you. Besides, I think that people who know and respect you have confidence in your judgment whatever you do, and your lover's age is of relative unimportance to them, as long as they're mature enough not to feel threatened by people sharing something considered a little out of the norm. They'll know, as you do, that what is brought to a relationship in terms of caring and nurturing and character is much more important than the number of years a person has lived.

For any women about to enter an older-woman younger-man alliance, I have only one piece of advice, and even in that I am echoing much of what's been said here before: Be yourself at all times. Don't try to act younger than you are. The man isn't interested in that. If he wanted a young girl, he wouldn't be with you in the first place. All you can end up doing is making both of you look foolish. Acceptance of age to me means acceptance of self. It is not easy, but when you can do it, the rewards are tremendous. Look at me, a very conventional woman who has led, from all accounts, a most conventional life. And just once, I wasn't afraid to step out, to take a chance of getting my feet wet, and here I am living and enjoying some of the best years I've ever had. I consider that a gift.

Nancy: The woman must also have a solid sense of self-esteem. It's best if she can face her aging gracefully, with a sense of humor. I think it helps if your circle of friends is broad and diverse, with people you've both cultivated.

Know what you're doing and who you are. It takes two mature individuals to handle long-term commitments, and there's much more pressure on any relationship that falls outside the norm. There's a great deal of helping and reaching out to one another in these liaisons, and you're not self-conscious about giving. You're glad that because of your differences you're able to offer special things. It gives you a sense of warmth and security. The women's movement has made us all aware of alternatives, shown us that there are many possibilities within other life-styles. Trust your feelings and don't be afraid of going after what you want. Perhaps, for older-woman/younger-man pairings to succeed over a period of years, it's necessary for one or maybe both partners to have a certain spirit of rebellion. What's important to remember is that the man is with you for a reason, just as you're with him, and that it's this caring that has to be developed and nurtured.

Barbara: I believe Frank and I are coming to an end now, but I have no regrets. Perhaps more than anything else, this relationship has changed my feelings about who and what's appropriate for me, what I need or require to be happy. Because of it, I will certainly be interested in other men who just happen to be younger—which opens up a whole new area of who and what is eligible. Over the years, I have refused several younger-man relationships because of my own hang-ups, and I regret that now and wonder what was lost. I believe that it's necessary for the woman to have a strong sense of emotional balance and inner security before testing the waters, because there is no question she's going to have to call on it to be able to withstand the put-downs and remarks of others that she's being used or that she's an object of some derision. There will always be people who will try and turn you into a cliché or a stereotype, and you have to learn to see past them. Every relationship carries its own brand of fear. None of us likes to appear vulnerable; nobody wants to be rejected or deserted. But that doesn't mean we should be afraid to try something because we can't forecast how it's going to end. There are no forevers, no guarantees in anything. So I would say remain your own person, stay in the here and now, and take each day as it comes, enjoying what you have.

Penny: John has been the major love of my life. I didn't expect it, wasn't looking for it, it just happened, and I consider myself very lucky. I have never had anyone to share anything with before. It's so great to hear him say; "This is ours; we're married now." We talk about our feelings, about what's coming ahead, our life together. I will tell you something: When I was thirty-eight, my oldest daughter, who was eighteen, said; "Ma, I think you ought to start building a life for yourself. We're getting older and don't want to leave you sitting around with that 'man' (who happened to be their father). . . . I asked her how to go about this. I said that I'd worked and had come home every night to the same life for so many years. Where should I go? How did I meet other people? . . . And that's when I first admitted to myself out loud that there had to be something else to try for in life. That I couldn't sit around and regret the things that were, because what had happened, happened, and I didn't want to become bitter by reliving my past. I knew if I did, I'd probably end up like my husband—an alcoholic. So I gave myself a pep talk. I was no longer twenty, I was going to be forty, but it was okay. I'd had one life with my children and it was coming to an end. And that, too, was okay as long as I was willing to face up to what was. The important thing to hold on to was that I felt the same inside as I had when I was a girl: I had gotten older, but the feelings were the same. And I mustn't be afraid to take a chance on life.

I was scared when John first proposed. I asked him if he was sure it was the right thing for us. And he was so reassuring that I could find no reason to refuse. He said, "Why should I be without you? I love you and I like you. You're my best friend. Somewhere out there, there are people like us who are looking for others. We'll find them, you'll see. There's no reason why we shouldn't marry when we feel about one another the way that we do."

And I thought: He's right. There are people out there who'll accept us. There are others who are sharing what we've found. And so I said yes. And I've never looked back or regretted making that decision. Because, you know something—I never expected such happiness. This past year has been the best of my life.

No one spoke when Penny finished. Each participant seemed lost in her own reflections. It was Alice who broke the silence. "If anyone is considering an older-woman/younger-man relationship, I want to tell them, for heaven's sake do it. . . . Age carries no weight when it comes to feelings. Nor when it comes to love."

4

WHAT THE EXPERTS SAY

In 1745, Benjamin Franklin gave the following "Advice to a Young Man."

Eight Reasons to Marry an Older Woman

1. Because they have more Knowledge of the world, and their Minds are better stored with Observations; their Conversation is more improving, and more lastingly agreeable.

2. Because when Women cease to be handsome, they study to be good. To maintain their Influence over Men, they supply the Diminution of Beauty by an Augmentation of Utility. They learn to do a thousand Services, small and great, and are the most tender and useful of all Friends when you are sick. Thus they continue amiable. And hence there is hardly such a thing to be found as an old Woman who is not a good Woman.

3. Because there is no hazard of children, which irregularly produced may be attended with much inconvenience.

4. Because through more Experience they are more prudent and discreet in conducting an Intrigue to prevent Suspicion. The Commerce with them is therefore safer with regard to your reputation; and with regard to theirs, if the Affair should happen to be known, considerate People might be rather inclined to excuse an old Woman, who would kindly take care of a young Man, form his manners by her good Councils, and prevent his ruining his Health and Fortune among mercenary Prostitutes.

5. Because in every Animal that walks upright, the

Deficiency of the Fluids that fill the Muscles appears first in the highest Part. The Face first grown lank and wrinkled; then the Neck; then the Breast and Arms; the lower parts continuing to the last as plump as ever; so that covering all above with a Basket, and regarding only what is below the Girdle, it is impossible of two Women to know an old one from a young one. And as in the Dark all Cats are grey, the Pleasure of Corporal Enjoyment with an old Woman is at least equal and frequently superior; every Knack being by Practice capable of improvement.

6. Because the sin is less. The Debauching of a Virgin may be her Ruin, and make her Life unhappy.

7. Because the Compunction is less. The having made a young Girl miserable may give you frequent bitter Reflections; none of which can attend making an old Woman *happy*.

8th and lastly. They are so grateful!!!

On April 24, 1978, the following question and reply appeared in Dr. Joyce Brothers' syndicated column:

Dear Dr. Brothers: I'm a 40-year-old woman wildly attracted to a man of 25. He says he loves me and wants to marry me as soon as possible. I have no great wealth so I know he can't be after my money. Despite what my friends say, I truly believe he loves me for myself. Everyone I know is aghast at the thought. They keep telling me if I marry him the marriage would be doomed to failure. I've had a rather unhappy life, for many reasons I won't go into now, but this is one of the greatest things that's ever happened to my life. We have a marvelous sex relationship and I'm warned that this can't last. What do you think? Is he going to tire of me?

J.O.

Dear J.O.: He may, but then you may tire of him. This could be said of any man and any woman who marry. There are no guarantees for happiness, and I suspect your chances are good and in some ways better than those of a woman entering a marriage with a man who is slightly older.

Ask your friends what their reaction would be if it were a man marrying a younger woman. If they're honest, and they probably won't be, they'd have to answer that they'd find this less alarming.

It's an interesting fact of life that women at 40 are often at a sexual peak. The aging process needn't impair a woman's sexual pleasure or receptivity. You're probably much better matched sexually to this man than you would be if he were nearer your age. If you love him, celebrate. Be glad and ignore the advice of your friends.

So it seems that two hundred and forty-three years later the advice remains essentially the same (making allowances for Old Ben's male chauvinism and taking into account that no matter how advanced anyone is, he is still a product of his time).

The following experts in their fields are also products of the times. They don't always agree, but what they have to say is worthy of our attention.

ARE THESE COUPLES SEXUALLY COMPATIBLE?

When I wrote my book *Women and Sex*, I found that women's ideas about orgasm came from literature—they read this was the way they should have orgasm, and so be it. And yet all the talk about good sex and orgasmic peak doesn't matter at all. The number of times a person can or can't reach climax is not an accurate measure of how much that person enjoys his or her sexuality. It's the attitudes one holds toward sex that really count.

Dr. Leah Schaefer
Psychotherapist
Author, *Women and Sex*

I can't find anything in the anatomical or physiological literature to demonstrate that sexual peaks are biologically induced or that there are chemical imperatives. What happens is that we've been socialized to accept this statement as fact. I believe what happens is that women, by the time they're in their early thirties, have finally had enough sexual experience to know what they want. They know who they are and they know how they want it. Young men have always been encouraged to act out their sexual desires. It's always been expected of men. The way a man relates sexually in his twenties and thirties and forties is the best predictor of how he will relate in his fifties and sixties.

People can relate to each other sexually all through their life cycle if all physical systems are "go," if they're involved in a nurturing relationship, and if they get sufficient stimulation.

> Dr. Michael Carrera,
> Chairman of the Board of the Sex Information
> and Education Council of the United States

Older women are finding that younger men are more satisfying sexually—and in many cases, more exciting generally. This is because younger men are often less set in their ways and more liberal in their attitudes. Theoretically, there should be greater sexual compatibility. The male should be more liberated and experimental if he gets involved in the relationship, and in some cases he should be able to accept sexual assertiveness on the part of the female.

> Dr. Arline Rubin,
> Associate Professor
> Brooklyn College

The woman can enjoy a degree of satisfaction in being the leader, teacher, and preceptor, whether from the sexual or ex-

periential point of view. Masters and Johnson and Kinsey
have shown that the sexual appetites of a woman in her thirties are comparable to those of a man in his late teens. When
the woman forms a relationship with a man ten to fifteen
years her junior, more likely than not the sexual appetites of
the partners in question will coincide. There's apt to be a degree of gratitude, on the part of the younger man vis-à-vis the
older woman, which she might never have experienced with
her prior peer (or older) husband or lovers.

> Dr. Wayne Myers
> Clinical professor of psychology
> New York Hospital

IS AGING A PROBLEM?

Aging on the woman's part is not a problem. All the actuarial
statistics favor the woman. A young man marrying an older
woman might very well mean that these two companions can
experience the life trip together and end it at the same time.
The mating choice will be made on potential for companionship, rather than on superficial looks.

> Dr. Penelope Russianoff
> Clinical therapist
> Professor, New School for Social Research

The relationship might make the woman more conscious of
her aging, but that would be outweighed by the fact that she
is attractive to the man, that he wants her and desires to be

with her. On the other hand, she might worry because she can't compete with a younger woman, and on those occasions she would have to curb her jealousy.

Nena O'Neill
Coauthor, *Open Marriage*
Author, *The Marriage Premise*

Initially, an older-woman/younger-man pairing may contribute to a woman's sense of herself as youthful—but inevitably, telltale signs of age will appear. And unless one is on friendly terms with a plastic surgeon, the woman will invariably fear that the man may desert her for a younger mate. Aging is a problem, and the pains in this type of liaison are significant and not to be minimized.

Dr. Wayne Myers

Relationships are difficult enough to maintain when both parties are about the same age; but when one partner is considerably older, added difficulties usually ensue. Those who choose this option must feel free to consider the course of separation or divorce later on. What happens is that almost all pressures—family, children, peers, and career—are enhanced (except perhaps in special circumstances, as when the woman is wealthy). In addition, there is the criticism of friends and relatives to contend with, along with the different interests that usually accompany age differences. And for the woman there is the nagging worry about her fading looks. What will she look like in five years? How well will she age?

Dr. Albert Ellis, Author
President, Institute for Advanced
Study in Rational Psychotherapy

Whether or not the affair has a chance to survive the inherent problems depends largely on the woman's motivations for having an affair with a younger man. Is the woman unhappy at the thought of growing older? Or is she rejecting something in herself by shunning men in her own age group? Is the alliance a hurt reaction to breaking up with an older man? Or is it an outlet for a long-suppressed sexual desire for a younger brother? She must determine whether the affair is important to her for itself, or whether it's a symptom of a larger, possibly pathological need.

> Dr. William S. Appleton[1]
> Psychiatrist
> Columnist, *Cosmopolitan*

The older person usually contributes stability, experience, and accumulated knowledge; the younger person, energy, zest, and a sense of interest in new things. Putting these two forces in synergy can create a very dynamic relationship.

> Sam Julty
> Author, *Male Sexual Performance*

The misconceptions, fallacies, and even taboos directed toward the sexual functioning of women in menopausal and post-menopausal years are legion. Knowledge of natural variations in the female sexual cycle that develop with the aging process has been extremely limited. We must, in fact, destroy the concept that women in the 50–70 age group have no interest in and no capacity for active sexual expression. Nothing could be further from the truth than the often-expressed belief that aging women do not maintain a high level of sexual orientation.

> Masters and Johnson[2]

Results from questionnaires distributed to four thousand men, from *Beyond the Male Myth,* by Dr. Anthony Pietropinto and Jacqueline Simenauer[3]

Age does not matter at all	38.2%
The woman must be my age or younger	16.4%
The woman could be 5 years older, not more	16.3%
Age doesn't matter, but she must not look older	12.8%
The woman could be 10 years older, not more	11.3%
Prefer an older	3.0%
No answer	2.2%

WHY ARE OLDER-WOMAN/YOUNGER-MAN RELATIONSHIPS BECOMING MORE VISIBLE AT THIS TIME?

Women's Lib has triggered a lot of thinking in men. The smart man wants a mate who is a companion and, hopefully, an equal wage earner. For some men "the little dependent doll" will be replaced by a true companion, a person. The movement has redefined woman as capable of independence and self-enjoyment. She no longer "needs" a man in the old-fashioned sense. She derives much pleasure from her female friends. She is more interesting as a total person; neither seeing herself as just a sex object nor as the embodiment of the "mother" figure.

Dr. Penelope Russianoff

With the advent of the feminist movement, the whole issue of sexuality has opened up. Some women in their early twenties appear to their male peers so demanding that the men feel they've been frightened away. It's give me an orgasm, give me what I want, do what I say. It's me, me, me! But an older woman who has an acceptance of herself, a sense of maturity—that gives the younger man a lot more confidence than a contemporary with whom he'd have to prove himself.

Mildred Klingman
Psychiatric social worker

Women are allowing themselves to have relationships with younger men because it is now more acceptable than it once was. Older women are also divorcing more easily today and do not necessarily want to marry again.

Dr. Arline Rubin

Women are blooming as independent people. They are feeling much better about themselves, and for a man that's a turn-on. The chances of a man of twenty-five or thirty having a sexual relationship with someone, say, forty-five, twenty years ago, were not very great, but we now approach one another differently. We are more willing to share our thoughts person to person, rather than placing walls between. Many of the age barriers that were in existence years ago are no longer seen as constraining barriers for relationships.

Dr. Michael Carrera

WHAT DOES THE WOMAN GAIN?

The mating choice will be made on potential for companionship rather than on superficial looks. A woman who has not been chosen on "young looks" could age gracefully, letting her personality shine through—rather than spending hours with face lifts, special hair-dos and a gym.

Dr. Penelope Russianoff

There will no doubt be many an older woman who will be threatened by a younger man—whom she thinks will microscopically examine every aging sign just the way she does. But nowadays, for this same older woman, that may be the only game in town. The reason is that her male contemporary will not be interested in her unless he wants a replay of a former marriage. Instead, he has changed his pattern and is looking for a young, attractive girl—one who will make him feel young and attractive also. Consequently, older women cannot really find interesting attractive men around their own age.

Mildred Klingman

Women now are marrying younger men. Men formerly were able to trade off power for sex. Women should be able to trade off their power for the sexuality, power, and vigor of younger men.

Jean Lipman-Blumen[4]
Sociologist

The great appeal of the younger man to the older woman can be summed up in one word: EGO! A non-dragging and not-so-sagging body has got to be a trip to the moon without leaving the bedroom. The younger man's interest, moreover, in working with his woman to have her dress chicly and youthfully, while encouraging excursions to the health salon and beauty parlor in an effort to delay the appearance of wrinkles or graying hair, has got to be a welcome change from her former and older mate who looked upon such trips as "wasteful" or an inability, on her part, to grow old gracefully.

> Barry B. Wolff
> Executive vice-president
> Barbizon Modeling Schools International

WHAT DOES THE MAN GAIN?

It feels like younger men today get a lot more living done within a shorter period of time, so that with a lot of experience behind them in terms of emotional and sexual relationships, they're ready at a much earlier age to look at the possibilities of a deeper commitment regardless of age. Certainly, the older woman's experience and depth would be attractive to them, not just because they're looking for a mother figure, or looking for that kind of comfort, or looking for that kind of training ground (though all these may be present), but because the depth of experience and feeling is attractive and stimulating to them in a relationship.

Also, one of the pleasures for the man, and I am saying this very idealistically, might be having the epitome of everything that is female—for, hopefully, she would, with age, be more compassionate, more sensitive, have all the depth of feeling that should come from experience. I would think that for a younger man, an older woman would be a tremendous plus.

> Nena O'Neill

Men sometimes find it difficult to relate to women their own age, especially when the women are on their own path to liberation. Hence, a relationship with an older woman, already liberated in a number of areas, is seen as a port in the storm. In short, she's what a lot of men look for: she's mellowed, more relaxed about herself, more confident about her total being. She's been there, and she doesn't have to prove anything!

Sam Julty

The younger man sees in her [the older woman] a mellow, fascinating person. She has the wisdom of her years. She knows how to please and treat a man. She's a mature woman with self-assurance. She knows how to carry herself, and because she knows who she is, she has the time and patience to listen to her man. She has found her "look" and is extremely attractive. Her charm and poise and wit took time to develop. She can hold her own. She has a mystery, and she has much to offer to herself, her man, and her community.

Verta Mae Smart-Grosvenor[5]
Writer

I believe one of the great reasons for a special compatibility between older women and younger men is the fact that women, as a general rule, tend to be more giving as they grow older, while men remain essentially "takers," despite maturity. The man seeks elements of Mother in his mate, and if Mother was nothing else, she was older. The younger man feels his machismo threatened far less by leaning on an older woman than on one who is younger. The older woman, moreover, is far more comfortable in the role of taking care of him and providing emotional support. She also is far more adept than her younger counterpart at making him happy—soothing, comforting, and caring for him.

Barry B. Wolff

WHAT ARE THE SPECIAL PAINS AND
PRESSURES IN THIS TYPE OF RELATIONSHIP?

Of course, social pressures will be more prevalent in any type of unconventional relationship, whether older man/younger woman, black/white, gay.

The biggest hurdle for this type of couple would be dealing with the reactions of the children from a previous, more "conventional" marriage. Because of weird concepts and principles about sexuality, anyone past the age of forty is supposed to wrap their genitals in fine gauze and leave them in a trunk in the attic along with other memorabilia. Many grown children of older men and women bring pressure against their parents having any sexual and/or romantic involvements at all. The pressure would be greater on the older woman than it has been for older men. Peers will sneer for the same reason children sneer when their best friend has a popsicle. Jealousy can take many forms.

Sam Julty

Some younger men may be less afraid of a quasi-mother figure than they are of a woman who is on an equal-to-equal footing, one who is comparable in age. For these men, another way of dealing with their fear of women who are their equals, is to ignore them and choose a substitute mother rather than a male. One element of homosexuality is a fear of the opposite sex—and choosing a substitute mother rather than a male might be another way of dealing with that fear.

If the homosexual element is not an issue, the younger man might still have a lot of anxiety about the son-mother relationship, and he would have to work this out before attempting a successful ongoing relationship with an older woman. If the man's relationship with his own mother hasn't been worked out, there's a very real possibility of too much transference taking place.

Dr. Leah Schaefer

We're much more accepting of the father-daughter relationship than of the prototypical mother-son relationship which is fraught with more complications and is more threatening to other people. The woman might become more of an adviser and mentor than a partner. And the younger man might become a "kept" man. The people involved might become victims to the stereotype—the woman abandoned for a younger woman, a woman with whom her lover or husband could have kids if he wanted them.

Nena O'Neill

If the older-woman/younger-man relationship were to result in marriage, there would be a great deal of static from the man's mother. Her acceptance would come slowly, if at all. If the woman were near her age, the mother would feel in competition with the wife. A mother's self-image is threatened unless her son marries well, gives her grandchildren, makes her feel like a successful mother. Looking at this type of relationship, she might very well say to herself: "Where did I go wrong?"

Mildred Klingman

There are special pains in this type of relationship, and I think they seem mostly to be related to criticism—particularly from the woman's children by a previous marriage. The man is regarded as a "fool." ("Young and fresh" win premium points in our culture; and every man, no matter what *his* age, is entitled to whatever he wants in the way of a woman.) So his friends and family regard him as throwing away opportunities if he chooses an older woman.

Dr. Penelope Russianoff

Probably the two most common ones experienced are the trauma to one's sense of self-esteem, which the woman often experiences when such liaisons don't work, and the inevitable social pressures. If a woman divorces her husband and takes up with a younger man, she's subjected to enormous pressures from her peers or from women slightly her senior. The Oedipal overtones of such condemnations are quite startling. It takes a brave woman and a strong relationship to withstand such pressure.

Nor are the younger men in these relationships immune to censure—especially in small towns where they have grown up and are known. It would certainly be here that they are subjected to intense familial and peer pressures. Few are sufficiently strong to withstand such challenges, and this often leads to denouncement and breakup. Sometimes the couple in point moves to another setting, often a large city, which is by nature more anonymous.

Dr. Wayne Myers

This type of relationship is usually uncongenial for having children, since the older woman may be less fertile, and the younger man (if he is very young) may not have much money. In addition, children from another union may see a younger man as a greater competitor for their mother than an older man. They may feel resentful. They may be bothered by anything that is nonconformist or unusual.

Dr. Arline Rubin

The danger of a May-December liaison is that the older woman will lie to herself, delude herself, and go into a decline when it's over. If you can accept the current moment and not program the future (which is very difficult), you will be all right. It's when you hang in for dear life, visit the plastic surgeon, pump vitamins into your stomach, and starve yourself into a beanpole that the relationship becomes harmful.

> Louise Montague[6]
> Author, *A New Life Plan*

Like it or not, people in different decades tend to have different priorities, which often lead to pressures few affairs can survive. Another potential problem, though strictly social, can be major: There's almost bound to be a gap between your lover and your friends, who may be more tolerant than enthusiastic when it comes to having a much younger man in their midst.

> Dr. William S. Appleton[7]
> Columnist, *Cosmopolitan*

Older women feel a little lonely with younger men. There is a lot of explaining to do. People like to talk to someone who has shared similar experiences, who come from the same reference points, and who can communicate without confusion.

> Janet Gifford
> Career consultant

The man is experiencing what the woman has already gone through in her life (in situations and feelings), and she can feel a gulf between them—a distance. The younger man may lose interest as the older woman visibly ages faster than he does, perhaps years after the relationship has begun.

Adele Nudel[8]
Author, *For the Woman over 50*

IS THE OLDER-WOMAN/YOUNGER-MAN
RELATIONSHIP A VIABLE
OPTION FOR THE FUTURE?

If it's a good relationship, then it's a good relationship and the age difference won't matter.

Mildred Klingman

In all probability these relationships will alter society's idea of aging. People tend to think of older people as those over the hill . . . that only younger people deserve the goodies of all kinds. Older women/younger men is viable because it breaks a common stereotype, and anything that opens up people's choices is a forward trend.

Dr. Leah Schaefer

With women outliving men from four to six years, it makes sense to marry a younger man.

Ann Landers[9]
Syndicated advice columnist

This is another high-risk relationship that can work beautifully—or not work at all. It depends on how reality-based you are, and what your expectations are and how much you need the approval of other people (how autonomous you are).

Adele Nudel[10]

In some ways, couples will be more compatible because they've specifically chosen one another against social and cultural mores and odds. And now the challenge is there for them to try and make it together in spite of the odds. Presumably, they've thought long and well about the relationship and decided in its favor on good grounds.

Dr. Albert Ellis

Older-woman/younger-man pairings can be very beautiful. So many isms have kept us away in the past (race, religion, age, etc.). As these artificial barriers fall down, people can afford to be people with each other rather than being labeled as this man or this woman who just happens to be out of reach for any sensitive relationship because they're twenty years older or younger. We are starting to see people in these relationships as two human beings; people who care for and about one another.

Dr. Michael Carrera

I support any relationship which is *loving and co-operative*. For many men, relating with an older woman can be just that. The point is, who is anyone to say the relationship is good or bad except the two people involved?

Sam Julty

AFTERTHOUGHTS

We believe that every important act involves taking some degree of risk. We consider the people you've come to know on these pages and the many more who shared their time and lives with us as special. These were not stereotypical relationships in which the woman was buying companionship and sex and the man was searching for his mother, but rather, well-thought-out and serious commitments for both partners. While we do not advocate these pairings for everyone, we do see it as an ever-increasing *option* for men and women.

Since the men were more reluctant to speak with us, we can only surmise that they felt outnumbered by having to talk to two women or that there truly is a role division that allows women to verbally explore their relationships and emotions in greater depth than men.

The men we did talk to, and those whose attitudes were conveyed to us by the women we came to know, seemed on the whole to have one thing in common: The majority of them did not want or feel the need to have their own children. They were perfectly willing to give up the idea of ever becoming biological fathers.

We also found that numerous people chose to cross over familial, religious, or racial lines to be with the person they loved. It appeared that if they crossed one societal taboo, then they would just as likely cross another.

At the beginning of this book we posed the question of what was meant by the term "older woman/younger man." The responses to our inquiries and questionnaires have indicated that age, like beauty, is all in the eye of the beholder. And, during our many interviews, we did indeed meet people whom we considered to be "age-free." Older women and younger men sought each other out for a wide variety of reasons. It seemed to us that the veneer—the whys and wherefores—didn't matter. What was important was the nature of the relationship and the feelings of the people involved.

For our culture to move forward in positive directions we need to banish the myths surrounding anything that is different. We need to free ourselves of what the poet William Blake called "mind-forged manacles."

In the May 29, 1978, issue of *People* magazine, there were stories on James Coburn, age fifty, artist Saul Steinberg, sixty-three, actor Brett Halsey, forty-four, and maestro Georg Solti, sixtyish. Each was either living with or married to a woman at least twenty years younger than himself. Not once in any of the articles was the age difference commented upon. It was merely mentioned as a fact in passing.

We look forward to the day when a woman who is living with a man significantly younger is also no longer put through the third degree; when she's not asked if the relationship has a chance of lasting, or what benefits they both bring to it. . . . When she and the man in her life can just relax and enjoy one another because the pairing is no longer considered newsworthy. That will be progress.

APPENDIXES

In a January 1978 article in the New York *Times Book Review*, Francine du Plessix Gray bemoaned the fact that there was a dearth of American and British fiction dealing with the older-woman/younger-man theme. And yet, she continued, this liaison is abundantly replayed in the classics of European literature. There is Madame Bovary, by Flaubert, and Madame de Vionnet in *The Ambassadors*. Among the other books she mentions are Goethe's *Werther*; Benjamin Constant's *Adolphe*; Choderlos de Laclos's *Les Liaisons Dangereuses*; Stendhal's *The Red and the Black*; Flaubert's *Sentimental Education*; many of Balzac's novels and novellas; notably *Lost Illusions*; Daudet's *Sapho*; Italo Svevo's *When a Man Grows Older*; Françoise Sagan's *Aimez-vous Brahms?*; and most particularly the work of Colette.

We go to movies and to the theater for purposes of information, entertainment, and escape. We also read for these same reasons. Subjects that were once taboo are now treated to full exposure in your favorite neighborhood movie theater or in the book rack of your local supermarket. It is then left up to the viewer, or to the reader, to either reinforce an old belief, accept the new concept as interesting and viable, or negate its existence in his or her life.

Many of us tend to denigrate anything that is in some way unusual, out of the ordinary, or not within our social context. New ideas, particularly those that affect life-styles and relationships, are often seen as a threat to the status quo and a reflection on our own sense of personal security. The more exposure that older-woman/younger-man relationships get—be they portrayed in print or on the screen—the more we will be forced to re-evaluate and sometimes relinquish our long-held, once-cherished beliefs about how we live and behave.

CURRENT BOOKS

In Erica Jong's How to Save Your Own Life (Holt, Rinehart & Winston), we have the heroine, best-selling author Isadora Wing, leaving her Chinese psychiatrist husband, moving to Hollywood, and falling madly in love with Josh, a man six years her junior.

November, December, by George Bower (Dutton), chronicles the growth of a boy to young manhood. During his time of passage, he meets, falls in love with, and then is left by, an older woman.

David Storey's novel is set in a Yorkshire mining community during the years just before World War II and moving into the fifties. The Saville family pin their hopes and dreams on Colin, their eldest son. And it is his story of coming of age—his friendships, school days, first romance, and love affair with a married older woman—that is reflected so powerfully in Saville (Harper & Row).

Sheila is the upper-middle-class wife in Brian Moore's novel The Doctor's Wife (Farrar, Straus & Giroux). When her husband cannot accompany her to France for what is supposed to be a second honeymoon, she goes alone and falls in love with Tom, an American boy years younger.

Joanna Banana could have been anything: an actress, singer, playwright. Instead, she became a New Jersey wife and mother of three. At forty-five, Joanna discovers she's "gotten old without hardly doing anything." And so, in running fantasies, she divorces and remarries a twenty-six-year-old. Her story is told by Bonnie Bluh in Banana (Macmillan).

Frank MacShane's biography The Life of Raymond Chandler (Dutton) records this American-born, British-educated creator of Philip Marlowe, the hard-boiled detective. We learn that Chandler, who drank himself out of a business career, began writing only at the age of forty-five, while married to a woman twenty years his senior.

Nora, the heroine of Edna O'Brien's I Hardly Knew You (Doubleday), is intelligent, talented, and beautiful. And yet we meet her in a prison cell, where she is being held for questioning in the murder of a young student named Hart. Through a series of memories and dreams, we learn of her family, husband, and unquenchable pursuit of men. With Hart, a man half her age, she thinks she has found her perfect love. And, on reflection: "Of course I would go with him, I would be mad not to. Not to fill the common rut of days with some fleeting suggestion of Happiness."

Doris Lessing's *The Summer Before the Dark* (Knopf) describes Kate Brown's movement into middle age. Wife of a London neurologist and mother of four children, she finds herself at forty-five questioning her very being. Who is she? What is she? Has she lost her sexuality? She seeks the answers by journeying alone to the Continent, where she meets and has an affair with a thirty-two-year-old American named Jeff Merton.

Helen Van Slyke, the author of *The Best Place to Be* (Doubleday), involves her widowed heroine, Sheila, in a love affair with a younger man. In the following passage, Sheila's daughter-in-law surprises her by offering support rather than by moralizing about the relationship:

> " . . . Who made up rules about right and wrong? 'Society' says it's wrong for a woman to enjoy the company of a man younger than herself, even though it's all right for any old duffer to take out a girl young enough to be his daughter. Nobody thinks *that's* disgraceful, in fact it's almost expected. Nobody gets all hung up about *his* sensibilities if the girl drops him for whatever reason. I suppose they think he can replace her without blinking an eye or shedding a tear. It seems to presume that the male is the stronger sex emotionally as well as physically, and I have my doubts about *that*. You know I'm no big Libber, Sheila, but this is one double standard I can't swallow. Why should people condemn you for seeing a man who's not your age? What the hell's wrong with that? I know a lot of guys who like more mature, experienced women, 'real' fellas in their thirties who're bored to death with the aimless chatter of dames my age. And lately, young women are so competitive, so hell-bent on being 'equal' that more and more young guys are realizing that it's exciting to be with a really feminine female. One like you, who isn't out to castrate them. One who knows how to make a man feel strong and protective. That kind of knowledge comes with experience, and you don't get that experience—socially and sexually—when you're two years out of college. The whole damn system is cockeyed! . . . Dammit, Sheila, if you and Jerry are finding something you need in each other, who's to say that isn't the thing to do?"

Master storyteller Isaac Bashevis Singer writes his spiritual autobiography as a young man growing up in Warsaw, Poland, in the twenties and thirties. In *A Young Man in Search of Love* (Doubleday), he describes the memorable character of Gina, ". . . perhaps twice as old as I but a woman whom I could love and from whom I could learn."

Six Months with an Older Woman (Avon), by David Kaufelt, is the love story of a thirty-year-old single swinger and the woman who taught him how to love. Isobel, the object of his affection, is a forty-five-year-old divorcee with two children.

THEATER

Tea and Sympathy, by Robert Anderson. Deborah Kerr offers more than both to the young man (John Kerr) that her husband, the headmaster of the prep school, accused of being homosexual.

Sweet Bird of Youth, by Tennessee Williams. Aging film actress (Geraldine Page) picks up young knockabout with acting pretensions (Rip Torn) with promise of pushing his career in Hollywood. He runs into a former girl friend in a small southern town and after many complications and much violence leaves the actress for her.

Forty Carats, by J. Allen. Forty-year-old divorcee (Julie Harris) falls in love with twenty-two-year-old while her daughter falls in love with a man old enough to be her father. Ending insinuates both affairs will turn out well; i.e., in happy marriages.

MOVIES

Smouldering Fires, 1925, Universal, directed by Clarence Brown. Successful businesswoman (Pauline Frederick) at forty has had no time for romance or marriage. Meets and falls in love with a young male employee at the factory she manages. They marry, but the difference in age is a constant barrier. He falls in love with her younger sister (Laura LaPlante), and the wife, realizing the hopelessness of the situation, asks for a divorce, pretending she no longer loves him, clearing the way for the young couple.

Devil in the Flesh, 1949, (French), A.F.E. Corporation, directed by Claude A. Lara. During World War I a high school student (Gérard Philipe) falls in love and has an affair with an older, married woman (Micheline Presle), ending with death of the latter.

Sunset Boulevard, 1950, Paramount, directed by Billy Wilder. Once-famous silent-film star, now an eccentric recluse (Gloria Swanson), hires a young writer (William Holden) to work on script for her return to the screen. She falls in love with him, becomes possessive and jealous, then shoots him when he attempts to leave her.

All About Eve, 1950. Broadway star Margo Channing (Bette Davis) is threatened professionally and personally by younger actress Eve Harrington (Anne Baxter).

Cast a Dark Shadow, 1957, (British), Dist. Corp. of America, directed by Lewis Gilbert. Psychotic young man (Dirk Bogarde) marries a well-to-do woman many years his senior (Mona Washbourne), then plots her murder.

Room at the Top, 1959, Continental, directed by Jack Clayton. Unscrupulous young man (Laurence Harvey), determined on wealth and position through rich young girl (Heather Sears), also has affair with older, married woman (Simone Signoret who received an Oscar for her performance), then throws her over when she no longer fits into his scheme of things. Signoret is killed in an auto accident as Harvey leads Sears to the altar.

The Roman Spring of Mrs. Stone, 1961, Warner's, directed by Jose Quintero. Aging actress (Vivien Leigh) arrives in Rome after death of her husband and falls in love with young gigolo (Warren Beatty), who later insults and leaves her for a younger woman (Jill St. John), whereupon the actress invites into her apartment a mysterious young man (Death?) who has pursued her throughout the film. (Adapted from Tennessee Williams novel.)

The Idol, 1966, Embassy, (British), directed by Daniel Petrie. Possessive mother (Jennifer Jones) is seduced by young friend (Michael Parks) of her son (John Leyton), who becomes enraged when he finds out, and causes death of Parks.

The Graduate, 1967, Embassy, directed by Mike Nichols. Innocent college graduate (Dustin Hoffman) is taught the ways of life and love by older woman (Anne Bancroft), a friend of his parents he meets at a party. She becomes intensely jealous when he transfers his attentions to her daughter (Katherine Ross).

The Gypsy Moths, 1969, M-G-M, directed by John Frankenheimer. Three barnstorming skydivers come to home town of one of them, whose aunt (Deborah Kerr) is smothered by loveless marriage and small-town life. She has brief affair with another of the daredevils (Burt Lancaster), who is killed in attempting new stunt. She elects to remain with husband.

Summer of '42, 1971, Warner's, directed by Robert Mulligan. Fifteen-year-old boy (Gary Grimes) is attracted to the wife (Jennifer O'Neill) of a World War II serviceman. When she receives word of her husband's death, she allows herself to be comforted by the boy and has a one-night affair with him, then leaves a note wishing him well.

The Last Picture Show, 1971, Columbia, directed by Peter Bogdanovich. In small Texas town, a high school senior (Timothy Bottoms) has affair with middle-aged wife (Cloris Leachman) of school coach. He then romances and attempts to marry young girl (Cybill Shepherd), whose mother represses her own sexual feelings toward him. After many troubles, Bottoms returns to Leachman for sympathy and understanding at picture's end.

Harold and Maude, 1971, directed by Hal Ashby. Maude (Ruth Gordon), eighty, is the spry older woman who teaches twenty-year-old, death-obsessed Harold (Bud Cort) how to live and love.

Ali, (European title: *Fear Eats the Soul*), c. 1974, released here by New Yorker Films, directed by Rainer Werner Fassbinder. Munich widow in her sixties (Bridgitte Mira) goes into an Arab bar to get out of the rain. Meets thirty-year-old Moroccan worker named Ali (El Hedi ben Salem). They have an affair and later marry, to the horror of their families and friends, who begin a systematic "persecution" of the two. In spite of many troubles (at one point, he is unfaithful), they remain together, and the unresolved ending insinuates that— given half a chance—the relationship may succeed.

Moment by Moment, 1978, Universal, directed by Jane Wagner. Trisha (Lily Tomlin), a bored rich housewife living in a Malibu beach house, and Strip (John Travolta), a car jockey turned beach bum, meet and fall in love.

NOTES

INTRODUCTION

1. New York *Times* interview, "Lynn Fontanne at 90," by Judy Klemesrud, April 24, 1978.
2. Alfred C. Kinsey, W. B. Pomeroy, and C. E. Martin, *Sexual Behavior in the Human Male* (Philadelphia: W. B. Saunders, 1948); Alfred C. Kinsey et al., *Sexual Behavior in the Human Female* (Philadelphia: W. B. Saunders, 1953).
3. Gail Sheehy, *Passages* (New York: E. P. Dutton, 1976), The Sexual Diamond.
4. Ibid.
5. Dr. Mary Jane Sherfey, *The Nature and Evolution of Female Sexuality* (New York: Vintage Books, 1973).
6. Barbara Seaman, *Free and Female* (New York: Coward-McCann & Geoghegan, 1972).
7. Ashley Montagu, *The Natural Superiority of Women* (New York: Macmillan, 1968).
8. *People* magazine, May 16, 1977.
9. New York *Daily News*, September 1978.
10. *Newsday Sunday Magazine*, July 10, 1977.
11. *Newsweek*, October 24, 1977, pp. 84–85.
12. William H. Masters and Virginia E. Johnson, *Human Sexual Response* (Boston: Little, Brown, 1966).
13. Nancy Mayer, *The Male Mid-life Crisis* (New York: Doubleday, 1978).

THE PEOPLE INVOLVED

1. Lance Morrow, "In Praise of Older Women," *Time* magazine, April 24, 1978.

FROM A MALE POINT OF VIEW

1. Paul Theroux, "Bewitched by Older Women," *Playboy* magazine.
2. Donald S. Marshall, *Ra'ivavae: an Expedition to the Most Fascinating and Mysterious Island in Polynesia* and Marshall and Suggs, "Sexual Behavior of Mangaia" (New York: Doubleday, 1961).

3. New York *Times,* January 14, 1977.
4. Francine du Plessix Gray, *The New Older Woman,* New York *Times Book Review,* January 15, 1978.
5. Interview with authors.
6. Interview with authors.

THE WOMEN SPEAK

1. Alvin Toffler, *Future Shock* (New York: Random House, 1974).
2. Shere Hite, *The Hite Report* (New York: Macmillan, 1976).
3. Ibid.

WHAT THE EXPERTS SAY

1. Dr. William S. Appleton, "Analyst's Couch," *Cosmopolitan* magazine, September 1977.
2. William H. Masters and Virginia E. Johnson, *Human Sexual Inadequacy,* (Boston: Little, Brown, 1970).
3. Dr. Anthony Pietropinto and Jacqueline Simenauer, *Beyond the Male Myth,* (Times Books, 1977).
4. Jean Lipman-Blumen, cited in column, by Georgie Anne Geyer, "She Confesses—She's Not Attracted to Young Boys," Chicago *Sun-Times,* 1978.
5. Verta Mae Smart-Grosvenor, quoted by Lynn Norment in "Older Women—Younger Men," *Ebony* magazine, May 1978.
6. Louise Montague, *A New Life Plan: A Guide for the Divorced Woman,* (New York: Doubleday, 1978).
7. Dr. William S. Appleton, op. cit.
8. Adele Nudel, *For the Woman over 50,* (New York: Taplinger, 1978).
9. Column in Newark *Star Ledger,* 1976.
10. Op. cit.

BIBLIOGRAPHY

1. Chesler, Dr. Phyllis. *About Men*. New York: Simon & Schuster, 1978.
2. Davitz, Joel; and Davitz, Lois. *Making It from 40 to 50*. New York: Random House, 1976.
3. Eisner, Dr. Betty Grover. *The Unused Potential of Marriage and Sex*. Boston: Little Brown, 1970.
4. Erikson, Erik H. *Identity, Youth and Crisis*. New York: W. W. Norton, 1968.
5. Farrell, Warren. *The Liberated Man*. New York: Random House, 1974.
6. Fuchs, Estelle. *The Second Season*. New York: Doubleday, 1977.
7. Harris, Janet. *The Prime of Ms. America*. New York: G. P. Putnam's Sons, 1975
8. Hite, Shere. *The Hite Report*. New York: Macmillan, 1976.
9. Hunt, Morton. *Sexual Behavior in the 1970's*. Chicago: Playboy Press, 1974.
10. Janeway, Elizabeth. *Between Myth and Morning: Women Awakening*. New York: William Morrow, 1974.
11. Kaplan, Helen. *The New Sex Therapy*. New York: Brunner/Mazel, 1974.
12. Komisar, Lucy. *The New Feminism*. New York: Franklin Watts, 1971.
13. LeShan, Eda. *The Wonderful Crisis Of Middle Age*. New York: David McKay, 1973.
14. Masters, William H.; and Johnson, Virginia E. *Human Sexual Response*. Boston: Little, Brown, 1966. *And Human Sexual Inadequacy*. Boston: Little, Brown, 1970.
15. Mayer, Nancy. *The Male Mid-life Crisis*. New York: Doubleday, 1978.
16. Montagu, Ashley. *The Natural Superiority Of Women*. New York: Macmillan, 1968.
17. Montague, Louise. *A New Life Plan: a Guide for the Divorced Woman*. New York: Doubleday, 1978.
18. Nudel, Adele. *For the Woman over 50*. New York: Taplinger, 1978.
19. O'Brien, Patricia. *The Woman Alone*. New York: Quadrangle/New York Times, 1973.
20. Pietropinto, Dr. Anthony; and Simenauer, Jacqueline. *Beyond the Male Myth*. New York: Times Books, 1977.

21. Pleck, Joseph; and Sawyer, Jack (eds.). *Men and Masculinity.* Englewood Cliffs, N.J.: Prentice-Hall, 1974.
22. Safilios-Rothschild, Constantina. *Love, Sex, and Sex Roles.* Englewood Cliffs, N.J.: Prentice-Hall, 1977.
23. Seaman, Barbara. *Free and Female.* New York: Coward-McCann & Geoghegan, 1972.
24. Shanor, Dr. Karen. *A Study of the Sexual Fantasies of Contemporary Women.* New York: Dial Press, 1977.
25. Sheehy, Gail. *Passages.* New York: E. P. Dutton, 1976.
26. Sherfey, Dr. Mary Jane. *The Nature and Evolution of Female Sexuality.* New York: Vintage Books, 1973.
27. Singleton, Mary Ann. *Life After Marriage: Divorce as a New Beginning.* New York: Dell Publishing, 1977.
28. Sontag, Susan, "The Double Standard of Aging," *Saturday Review,* September 23, 1972.
29. Taves, Isabella. *Women Alone.* New York: Funk & Wagnalls, 1968.
30. Toffler, Alvin. *Future Shock.* New York: Random House, 1970.
31. Weideger, Paula. *Menstruation and Menopause.* New York: Alfred A. Knopf, 1976.
32. Wilson, Angela, "Can a 40-Year-Old Woman Find Happiness with a 29-Year-Old-Man?" *Ms.* magazine, June 1976.